Praise for *The 3D Lead*

M000205187

'A brilliant and practical must-read f[...]

Alex Amouyel, Executive Director, Massachusetts
Institute of Technology (MIT)

'A timely practical guide to being a bolder, braver and better leader in an age of relentless change and challenge.'

Megan Reitz, Professor of Leadership,
Hult International Business School; best-selling
author of Speak Up

'An extremely practical and well thought-through guide book for tomorrow's leader.'

John Sanei, best-selling author of What's
Your Moonshot? *and faculty member of*
Singularity University

'Put simply, Terence Mauri is a brilliant thinker. This book assembles clever insight and practical action into bold "future ready" leadership.'

Jamil Qureshi, performance coach to
six world number ones

'Leaders worth following are capable of leading people somewhere better, and this needs leaders who can accelerate their own learning in the practical, powerful ways Mauri sets out in his toolkit for 3D leadership.'

Dr Max McKeown, strategic psychologist;
author of The Strategy Book

'The leaders of today need to read *The 3D Leader* if they want to be the leaders of tomorrow.'

Tom Kegode, Senior Innovation Culture and
Capability Lead, Lloyds Banking Group

'Inspiring and instantly practical.'

Tendayi Viki, Associate Partner, strategyzer; author of
The Corporate Startup

'A powerful and instantly practical toolkit for maximising your leadership potential.'

Stuart Crainer, co-founder, Thinkers50

'Want to be a 10x leader? This book will show you how!'

Yannick Theler, founder and Managing Director,
Ubisoft Abu Dhabi

'The greatest compliment I can pay Terence Mauri's work is that he has the rare talent of being able to make you pause, reflect and think. His considered analysis, innovative thinking and entertaining and accessible writing make this latest book a triumph.'

Professor Damian Hughes, best-selling author of
The Barcelona Way

'Inspiring and thought-provoking read from an influential thinker.'

Benjamin Laker, Professor of Leadership, Henley
Business School

'Terence Mauri shows you how thinking bigger, bolder and better transforms the way today's leaders lead their people. A must-read on every leader's list.'

Ricardo Vargas, Executive Director, Brightline Initiative

'A must-read for all leaders aspiring to reach not just 10%, but 10x, growth in life and business.'

Annastiina Hintsa, CEO, Hintsa Performance

THE 3D LEADER

Pearson

Terence Mauri

THE 3D LEADER

TAKE YOUR LEADERSHIP TO THE NEXT DIMENSION

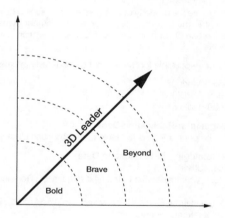

Pearson

Harlow, England • London • New York • Boston • San Francisco • Toronto • Sydney
Dubai • Singapore • Hong Kong • Tokyo • Seoul • Taipei • New Delhi
Cape Town • São Paulo • Mexico City • Madrid • Amsterdam • Munich • Paris • Milan

PEARSON EDUCATION LIMITED
KAO Two
KAO Park
Harlow CM17 9SR
United Kingdom
Tel: +44 (0)1279 623623
Web: www.pearson.com/uk

First edition published 2020 (print and electronic)
© Pearson Education Limited 2020 (print and electronic)

ISBN: 978-1-292-24837-0 (print)
      978-1-292-24838-7 (PDF)
      978-1-292-24839-4 (ePub)

British Library Cataloguing-in-Publication Data
A catalogue record for the print edition is available from the British Library

Library of Congress Cataloging-in-Publication Data
Names: Mauri, Terence, author.
Title: The 3D leader : take your leadership to the next dimension / Terence
   Mauri.
Description: First edition. | Harlow, England ; New York : Pearson, 2020. |
   Includes bibliographical references and index.
Identifiers: LCCN 2020012704 (print) | LCCN 2020012705 (ebook) | ISBN
   9781292248370 (paperback) | ISBN 9781292248387 (pdf) | ISBN
   9781292248394 (epub)
Subjects: LCSH: Leadership. | Organizational change.
Classification: LCC HD57.7 .M39348 2020 (print) | LCC HD57.7 (ebook) |
   DDC 658.4/092—dc23
LC record available at https://lccn.loc.gov/2020012704
LC ebook record available at https://lccn.loc.gov/2020012705

10 9 8 7 6 5 4 3 2 1
24 23 22 21 20

Cover design by Two Associates

Print edition typeset in Helvetica Neue LT W1G 9.5/13 by SPi Global
Printed by Ashford Colour Press Ltd, Gosport

NOTE THAT ANY PAGE CROSS REFERENCES REFER TO THE PRINT EDITION

To

My Father

CONTENTS

ABOUT THE AUTHOR

Terence Mauri is an *Inc.* Magazine writer, award-winning author, global keynote speaker and one of the most exciting business thinkers in the world who challenges leaders to own the future rather than be disrupted by it. His thinking has featured in *The Economist*, *Forbes*, Reuters, *HuffPost*, CNN and *Wired* and he has been described as 'an influential and outspoken expert on the future of leadership' by Thinkers50, the global ranking company of the top 50 management thinkers in the world.

www.terencemauri.com

www.thinkers50.com/blog/terence-mauri/

www.twitter.com/terencemauri

ACKNOWLEDGEMENTS

This book would not have been possible without the support of friends, family, delegates, mentors and clients. A huge thank you to my editor, Eloise Cook, and her award-winning team at Pearson/FT Publishing and to everybody who supported *The 3D Leader*'s publication, including Stuart Crainer, co-founder of Thinkers50, Yannick Theler, Founder and Managing Director of Ubisoft Abu Dhabi, Alex Amouyel, Executive Director, MIT, Megan Reitz, Professor of Leadership at Hult Business School and author of *Speak Up*, John Sanei, Singularity University, Jamil Qureshi, No.1 Coach in the world, Dr Max McKeown, author of *The Strategy Book*, Tom Kegode, Senior Innovation Culture & Capability Lead, Lloyds Banking Group, Tendayi Viki, Associate Partner at Strategyzer and author of *The Corporate Startup*, Julia Hobsbawm OBE, Dr Vicky Dondos, Professor Damian Hughes, author of *The Barcelona Way*, Professor Benjamin Laker, Henley Business School, Satya Nadella, Amanda Gilbert, Matt Hart, Morné Lippiatt, Sarah Christie-Rundle, Saana Azzam, Aymon Ansari, Rucha Roberts, Frances Keane, Tom Gregory, Sonia and Lucia Alice Mauri, Mike Lynch, Gennaro Mugnano, Nadia Petrik, Cosimo Turroturro, Rob Higgins, Veronique Plusjé, Maurice van der Kant, Peeyush Gulati, Ify Abraham, Andrea Snyder, Nancy Ventura, Rick Hoteck, Canesha Appleton, Steve Smith, Jonathan Stanger, Daniel McGonigle, Mollie Bloxsome, Allan Grant, Paul Warren, Siobhan Jackman, Lasse Rasmussen, Nello and Rita Mauri, Dania Al Tabbal and Mark Skinner.

A special thanks to the world-class teams at Thinkers50, *Inc.* Magazine, London Business School, MIT, Harvard Business School, Oxford University, London School of Economics, New York University, Wharton Business School, Raise The Bar Ltd, Maria Franzoni Ltd, A-Speakers Ltd, Personally Speaking Ltd, Chartwell Speakers Ltd, Speakers Associates Ltd, JLA Ltd, MENA Speakers Bureau, Lauranci Speakers Bureau and all the CEOs, delegates and clients I've had the fortune of working with and being inspired by over the years.

Finally, I'd like to thank Polona Pirnat for her magical illustrations in the book.

PUBLISHER'S ACKNOWLEDGEMENTS

15, 95, 119 McKinsey & Company: Adam Grant "Wharton's Adam Grant on the Key to Professional Success." McKinsey & Company; **24 American Psychological Association:** Marguc, J., Forster, J., & Kleef, G. A. V. (2011). Stepping back to see the big picture: When obstacles elicit global processing. Journal of Personality and Social Psychology, 101(5), 883–901. doi: 10.1037/a0025013; **43–44 Zhang Ruimin:** Zhang Ruimin's Haier Power: News: About Haier: Haier Group; **45 Microsoft Corporation:** Mission statement of Microsoft; **64 Hachette Book Group:** Schmidt, E., Rosenberg, J., & Eagle, A. (2015). Google: how Google works. London: John Murray; **65 TED Conferences, LLC:** Heffernan, M. (2015, December 7). The secret ingredient that makes some teams better than others; **78–80 Terence Mauri:** Mauri, T. (2019, September 17). Want to Thrive? Why This Leader Is on a Mission to Scale the Best Version of You. Used with permission from Terence Mauri; **79–80 Harvard Business School Publishing:** Catmull, E. (2019, February 25). How Pixar Fosters Collective Creativity; **83 Emilia Lahti:** Lahti, E. (2020, April 19). The Brilliance of a Dream: Introducing the Action Mindset. Used with permission from Emilia Lahti; **84 Rowling, J. K.:** Rowling, J. K. (2018, January 5). Text of J.K. Rowling's speech; **96 Guardian News & Media Limited:** Krotoski, A. (2010, March 14). Robin Dunbar: We can only ever have 150 friends at most; **97 IRISH TECH NEWS:** Cocking, S. (2019, February 6). Networking smarter, by Terence Mauri, author of The Leader's Mindset: How to Win in the Age of Disruption. Used with permission from Terence Mauri; **98 Guardian News & Media Limited:** Williams, Z. (2014, October 10). Julia Hobsbawm: 'I'm interested in social mobility, and I think there is a stuckness going on'; **102 Condé Nast:** Wolf, G. (2017, June 4). Steve Jobs: The Next Insanely Great Thing; **107 Penguin Random House:** Wiseman, R. (2011). The Luck Factor: The Scientific Study of the Lucky Mind. London: Cornerstone Digital; **108 Matthew Stafford:** Stafford, M. (2018, October 12). Building the Borderless Entrepreneurial Ecosystem. Used with permission from Matthew Stafford; **115–116 Penguin Random House:** Arbesman, S. (2012). The Half-Life of Facts: Why Everything We Know Has an Expiration Date. Penguin; **118–119 Harvard Business Publishing:** Snook, N. C. S. A. (2014, August 18). From Purpose to Impact;

120 Terence Mauri: Mauri, T. (2017, April 7). The Biggest Factor in Your Success? Finding Your 'Why'. Used with permission from Terence Mauri; **124 Liz Wiseman:** Liz Wiseman: Part 2 of an interview by Bob Morris. (2015, April 8); **125 Terence Mauri:** Mauri, T. (2018, February 28). Want to Get Ahead? Time to Find Yourself A Mentor. Used with permission from Terence Mauri.

CHAPTER 1

INTRODUCTION: THE CHALLENGE

We're here to put a dent in the universe. Otherwise, why else even be here?

Steve Jobs, Apple

In this chapter you will learn to:

- *unlock the 3D Leader System*
- *lead from the future*
- *understand the top 10 leadership trends*
- *complete the 3D Leader Test.*

HELLO TOMORROW

About six weeks ago, I received an email from somebody called Amy Ingram. It was a friendly, professional email to schedule a meeting with the CEO of an exciting new technology company I was researching for my Future Proof column in *Inc.* Magazine. After a couple of email exchanges, the meeting was confirmed and I thanked Amy for her time. When I got to meet with the CEO in person later that week in New York, he looked at me with a glint in his eye and asked, in a rather curious tone, 'What did you think of Amy Ingram's emails?' A little confused, I replied that they were very courteous and professional and, most importantly, achieved a good outcome. The CEO smiled again, paused and said that he had a confession to make: Amy was not a human being. She was, in fact, AI and the clue was in her initials (Amy Ingram). 'Will you forgive me?' he asked with a grin. My first reaction was embarrassment as I realised I hadn't been having a conversation with a human being. My second reaction was paranoia. I asked myself was I part of a Netflix Black Mirror film? My final reaction was that science fiction has become science fact. The future has already arrived: cars that drive themselves, platforms that can anticipate our every needs and robots capable of everything from advanced manufacturing to complex surgery. Of course, I did forgive the CEO, because everywhere around me I am seeing that the world is changing faster than at any point in human history, from the rapid spread of the Coronavirus (COVID-19) pandemic to climate change and the war for talent. Ernest Hemingway said change arrives in two ways – gradually and then suddenly. We live in a phy-gital world, a combination of physical and digital. As humans and machines increasingly work alongside each other, the day-to-day life of a leader will change drastically and, yet, most leaders don't have a clear view of the mindset and capabilities required to leverage these disruptive changes.

DISRUPTORS ON THE HORIZON

- Amazon just launched a credit card for the underbanked.
- Apple has launched a credit card with JPMorgan.

- Facebook is launching a cryptocurrency called Libra.
- Airbnb is moving into home loans.
- Microsoft is an AI-first company.
- Tesla is moving into insurance.

WHY THIS BOOK MATTERS

Consider this fact. Today is the *slowest* it will ever be in your lifetime. Technology will transform every facet of daily life, but are you ready for what that means for the future of work, leadership and success? And how can you galvanise, embolden and excite a new generation of thinkers, doers and change-makers? I believe the time has come to rethink and redefine what leadership means not just for today but for the 2020s and beyond.

To lead in this brave new world, you will have to find the courage to upgrade your mindset multiple times in order to remain viable and find the speed and agility to turn disruption into opportunity. The bad news is that you're probably not going to learn this at business school. Unexpected, rapid change is everywhere – and the greatest weapon against it is a radical shift in how leaders think and act because the current leadership model is broken. The World Economic Forum on the global outlook for 2020 identified lack of leadership as the number 1 challenge organisations will face over the next 12–18 months and, out of 1,767 respondents to the survey, 86% agreed there is a leadership crisis in the world today.

THE FACTS

1. 85% of employees globally are not engaged in their work (Gallup).
2. $900 billion is wasted on leadership training (Forbes).
3. 70% of largescale transformation efforts fail to meet all their goals (HBR).
4. 69% of what a manager currently does will be automated by 2024 (Gartner).
5. 60% of leaders have never been trained (Forbes).

There's something broken here: people are not doing their best work and that's because of poor leadership. I once had a terrible boss. His nickname in the office was 'silent assassin'. He wasn't the CEO but did hold a senior position as Head of Department for a big consultancy I worked at. I was in a windowless temporary office set up on his floor where I was asked to help get rid of 10% of employees owing to difficult trading conditions. The language used to describe this sorry state of affairs was obviously much more slick. 'Downsizing' was the term used, if I recall correctly.

My boss would make a show of coming in and out of my office, just staying for five minutes, practising his imaginary golf swing without saying a thing. Other times, I'd bump into him in the lift and he would just stand there with an unsettling death stare. No hello, no greeting, nothing. I started to ignore him. The rest of the team would watch him nervously, worried about who was going to be next. Once, he circled my desk menacingly and tapped his fingers along my shoulders like a keyboard, whispering in my ear, 'Mauri, I bet you're ready to bail, aren't you?' and then he'd snatch my phone and shout, 'Ah, there's a recruiter calling you back right now.' A psychopath boss, if ever there was one.

Reading this new book will help you do the following:

- Use a powerful and proven 3D Leader System to take your leadership to the next dimension.
- Unlock a new leadership mindset for learning, growth and change.
- Build a challenge culture where it's safe to speak up and bring your best and boldest self to work.
- Adapt to the extreme speed and complexity of change.
- Own the future rather than be disrupted by it.

TECHNOLOGY CHANGES FAST. HUMANS DON'T

A question for you. On a scale of 1–5 (5 = high), score how much the way you lead has changed in the last five years and how much you expect it will change in the next five years. What was the result? The chances are that you've got a low score for the first question and a high score for the second one. This is because technology changes quickly, but humans change much more slowly. Take meetings, for example, where the way they are run has not changed for more than 150 years or performance reviews that are often no more than tick-box exercises for many leaders. There are drawers full of strategies; the problem is most organisations aren't changing fast enough because their cultures, operating systems and processes are frozen in time. Remember that change is demanded from the outside but driven from the inside.

Times of rapid change and volatility call for a new leadership model. The greatest challenge facing many leaders is how to work in new, more nimble ways that are at odds with tried-and-true methods. This book is for anyone who wants to scale the best leader in themselves and their teams: this means you must leave your ego at the door, enable trust across teams, spark leadership at all levels and help make sense of disruption everywhere. Over the last 10 years, I've become fascinated by how leaders should respond when the future arrives faster than ever before. From studying the most inspiring companies and leaders around the world, I have discovered there are three leadership dimensions you must launch, scale and sustain in order to thrive, especially during a crisis: *bold*, *brave* and *beyond*. These are three action-oriented mindsets to simplify how you think, how you act and, ultimately, how you lead.

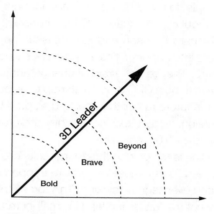

The 3D Leader

1. BOLD

- Think 10x, not 10%.
- Bold leaps.
- Break the rules.

Do you want to make the future or just react to the unknown? Make a list of leaders whom you admire and who have made a difference in the world. The chances are they all have one outstanding quality in common: they have the *bold* dimension. Barriers are there to be broken. Just look at the moment when history was made and the Kenyan runner Eliud Kipchoge ran a marathon in under two hours. That's an average of 100 m every 17 seconds, 422 times in a row! When was the last time you set a challenge for yourself that pushed you to deliver more than you thought was humanly possible? Most leaders think about how they can lead better by 10 or 20%, not by a factor of 10.

Bold is the first dimension of the 3D Leader System and excels at moonshots: taking bold leaps into the future. Imagine leading your organisation up to 10 times better than you do today or increasing your team's success tenfold. This is where the bold dimension can be really useful. *10x actions impact results at a much bigger scale.* 'Why be 10% better, when you could be 10 times better?' Ten times more profits, more customers, more quality, reduced cost, reduced time. Whatever. By giving yourself a 'How could we do it 10x better' challenge, you take a new perspective and solve problems in different ways.

There is no better time to disrupt than today. Leaders with the bold dimension are hardwired to think bigger and brighter, whether it's wiping out malaria in the next 10 years (the Bill & Melinda Gates Foundation), serving 2 billion people (former Alibaba CEO and founder Jack Ma), raising global awareness about climate change (Greta Thunberg) or making space tourism a reality (Richard Branson and Elon Musk). They have an eye on the future, flip threats into opportunities and can spot an unmet opportunity quickly before others. They're not afraid of change and enjoy bucking the norm. You don't have to be a CEO or run a startup to unlock this dimension; it's about owning the future rather than being disrupted by it. Get started, have a clear destination, fail fast, test ideas lightly and often, and know that those who are bold think 10x, not 10%.

The bold dimension is the golden thread that links great leaders around the world. The problem is that most leaders are trapped by legacy: legacy IT, legacy culture and even legacy thinking. This forces them to protect the past rather than invent the future and lead in small incremental ways, such as how to grow by 5% or 10% rather than 10x. Bold helps you thrive in uncertainty: it's a winning mindset, a way of thinking and acting that you can launch at any organisation.

2. BRAVE

- Speak up.
- Psychological safety.
- Choose courage over comfort.

Do you choose courage over comfort? *Brave* is the second dimension of the 3D Leader and is defined as the leader who 'brings their bravest selves to work, speaks up about problems, asks brave questions that cast aside old thinking, alerts others to concerns and challenges openly'. Compliance-focused organisations are no longer fit for purpose or even places where people want to work. Everybody has a brain and wants to use it everyday solving problems, helping customers and making a difference.

When's the last time you were brave as a leader? The brave dimension expands or shrinks in direct proportion to the daily courage you show when overcoming practical leadership challenges from boring meetings to old rules that need breaking. Like modern-day explorers ascending K2 or reaching the North Pole, I have discovered that at the core of the brave dimension is an action mindset, rooted in an ancient Nordic belief system called *sisu*. *Sisu* refers to 'extraordinary determination, courage and grit in the face of extreme stress or adversity'.

Every great leader I have met overcame battles that seemed insurmountable at the time and yet they did not give up. Where *sisu* flourishes, leaders and their teams report higher levels of psychological safety (safety to speak up, bring full self to work, share ideas and learn from failure), optimism (expecting good things to happen), feedback (commitment to helping others grow) and resilience (ability to adapt to obstacles and recover quickly).

The most innovative leaders are those who dare to step into the unknown, eliminate the unnecessary and get things done. The brave dimension is a leader's North Star for making tough decisions, stopping inertia and unlocking the huge benefits of what I call 'quantum teamwork'.

Quantum teamwork means excellence at every turn and is the sweet spot where psychological safety, cognitive diversity and trust intersect. The brave dimension is the key to tapping this superpower by giving everybody the freedom to bring their best selves to the job.

3. BEYOND

- Grow your networks.
- Walk your why.
- Be the change.

The novelist John Le Carré wrote that 'a desk is a dangerous place from which to view the world'. When's the last time you learnt something for the first time or stepped up to the challenge to go beyond the strategies and mindsets of today? *Beyond* is the final dimension of the 3D Leader System and is defined as 'how you lead yourself, make relationships, overcome your fears and go beyond your limits'. To do the impossible, you must replace fear with courage and navigate the rapid pace of change, activate your leadership purpose and *be* the change not just talk about change. The advantages are huge for any leader who can tap this dimension: harness your unique strengths, be an infinite learner, seize the best opportunities, walk your why and leverage your networks to thrive.

To scale the beyond dimension, think ABC. This stands for agile, bold and collaborative. Your team are there by choice. They can leave at any time. You may have chosen them, but every day they make a decision to remain part of the team. This is where most leaders make a big mistake. They forget that people want value and values – and a reason to work not just a place to work. The assumption is that once you have put the team in place, you can turn your attention away and focus your energies elsewhere. You can't do any of this alone. The beyond dimension demands leaders of change rather than leaders of continuity and is ultimately about being the leader you wished you had.

THE 3D LEADER TEST

Are you a 3D Leader? Take the test and identify your 3D Leader strengths and gaps.

Be honest with your answers and take the test again, once you've finished reading the book and you can see your scores go up. Even better, get somebody who knows you well to take the test on your behalf.

For each dimension, score your strength levels on a scale from 1 (low) to 10 (high). A score of 7 or below for each of the statements indicates a priority area for improvement.

BOLD DIMENSION

1. I have a bold vision of the future.

   1   2   3   4   5   6   7   8   9   10

2. I use failure as a rapid learning tool.

   1   2   3   4   5   6   7   8   9   10

3. I operate with a strong results orientation.

   1   2   3   4   5   6   7   8   9   10

4. I prototype ideas and test them quickly.

   1   2   3   4   5   6   7   8   9   10

5. I understand VUCA.

   1   2   3   4   5   6   7   8   9   10

6. I look outside my industry for inspiration.

   1   2   3   4   5   6   7   8   9   10

7. I am resilient in the face of setbacks.

   1   2   3   4   5   6   7   8   9   10

8. I understand the principles of 10x thinking.

   1   2   3   4   5   6   7   8   9   10

9. I think like an entrepreneur.

   1   2   3   4   5   6   7   8   9   10

10. I am a bold thinker.

   1   2   3   4   5   6   7   8   9   10

Bold total _____ / 10 =

BRAVE DIMENSION

1. I speak up about issues that matter.

1   2   3   4   5   6   7   8   9   10

2. I build psychological safety in my teams.

1   2   3   4   5   6   7   8   9   10

3. I give frequent, timely feedback.

1   2   3   4   5   6   7   8   9   10

4. I encourage constructive debate.

1   2   3   4   5   6   7   8   9   10

5. I hire for culture contribution.

1   2   3   4   5   6   7   8   9   10

6. I am committed to silo busting.

1   2   3   4   5   6   7   8   9   10

7. I build high trust teams.

1   2   3   4   5   6   7   8   9   10

8. I bring my best self to work.

1   2   3   4   5   6   7   8   9   10

9. I lead with empathy.

1   2   3   4   5   6   7   8   9   10

10. I ask brave questions.

1   2   3   4   5   6   7   8   9   10

Brave total _____ / 10 =

BEYOND DIMENSION

1. I use mentors to raise my game.

1   2   3   4   5   6   7   8   9   10

2. I am proactive at growing my networks.

1   2   3   4   5   6   7   8   9   10

3. I never stop learning.

1   2   3   4   5   6   7   8   9   10

4. I am passionately curious about the future.

1   2   3   4   5   6   7   8   9   10

5. I lead change.

1   2   3   4   5   6   7   8   9   10

6. I know my leadership strengths and blind spots.

   1   2   3   4   5   6   7   8   9   10

7. I have a clearly defined leadership purpose.

   1   2   3   4   5   6   7   8   9   10

8. I focus on my best work more than busy work.

   1   2   3   4   5   6   7   8   9   10

9. I think and act like a leader.

   1   2   3   4   5   6   7   8   9   10

10. I challenge the status quo.

   1   2   3   4   5   6   7   8   9   10

Beyond total _____ / 10 =

THE ANSWER

Fast-moving disruption requires a more fluid approach to leadership. What if leaders could tap into the underlying forces behind these kinds of changes and turn disruption into opportunity? Here are 10 leadership trends that are happening today that will require the leadership dimensions of *bold*, *brave* and *beyond* in order to succeed.

1. FROM MONEY TO MEANING

Economist Milton Friedman's original definition that the purpose of an organisation was solely to make profit for its shareholders no longer holds sway in a world with record levels of debt, climate change and loss of wildlife. The research is clear. According to IDEO's Purpose Index, people want a reason to come to work, not just a place to go and work and know that their work matters. The prize is 64% higher levels of engagement, 40% higher levels of retention and 13.4% higher levels of return on equity. Shareholder value is no longer everything. Leaders from Apple, JPMorgan Chase and Amazon have recently declared that they will place shareholders as just one of five stakeholders alongside customers, workers, suppliers and communities. This is long overdue but welcome because there's no plan B.

Are you exceeding, meeting or falling behind on your leadership purpose? Without purpose, it's impossible to innovate and challenge the shareholder-first mindset. Whether it's the best version of your organisation or the best version of your team, having the courage to lead on purpose is one of the best ways to win in the face of rapid change and uncertainty. Uncertain times require the certainty of purpose. Translate purpose all the way down to individuals and this will drive every part of an organisation's growth, learning and culture. Now meaning is the new money.

2. FROM COMPLEXITY TO SIMPLICITY

According to a recent McKinsey study, organisational complexity (number of procedures, structures, processes, systems, vertical layers and decision approvals) has increased by a factor of 35 in the last 6 years. Too much complexity is not only frustrating it can also waste time, erode productivity and kill growth. As our BMI (bureaucratic mass index) continues to rise, every leader must be committed to fighting complexity with simplicity.

How pervasive is bureaucracy in your organisation? How much time and energy does it suck up? To what extent does it undermine resilience, growth and innovation? Which processes are more trouble than they're worth? Today, business is inherently more complex than it has ever been. The moment you enter the office, you are suddenly exposed to a huge amount of rules, procedures and protocols. Now you have to empower everybody to replace complexity with simplicity in order to lead fast and stay relevant.

3. FROM HIERARCHIES TO NETWORKS

Ideas travel faster through networks than hierarchies and, yet, most organisations are still organised around outdated military models that are slow, risk averse and make decisions based on hierarchy. The best leaders know that innovation isn't a job title, a status or a department. It's a set of winning behaviours that should be spread, recognised and rewarded throughout the organisation. Strive to build a company of innovators rather than a department of innovation and a culture where people feel safe to speak up about things that matter.

Does your organisation suffer from HiPPO bias (highest paid person's opinion)? The HiPPO leader can shut down new solutions to old problems and new solutions to new problems because the team assumes the HiPPO always knows best. To combat HiPPO bias leaders have a duty of care to think differently about how meetings are run. For example, being the last person to speak and giving everybody time to collaborate and have meaningful conversations.

4. FROM EFFICIENCY TO INTELLIGENCE

If a picture paints a thousand words, an experiment can save a thousand meetings. Leaders must build challenge cultures where teams are empowered to turn ideas into impact and intelligent failure is a badge of honour rather than a badge of shame. The 3D Leader falls in love with problems and then makes small bets and cheap experiments to test whether the idea is viable or not. Amazon founder Jeff Bezos says every leader has a duty to build a culture where it's the best place in the world to fail. *What this means is that, if you don't systematically design your culture, two thirds of it will end up being accidental.*

What's your ROI? Not return on investment but return on intelligence and return on ideas. Most leaders still prioritise efficiency before experimentation and reward doing the things rather than doing the right thing. Whereas the nineteenth and twentieth centuries were defined by scaling efficiency, I believe leaders will have to prioritise intelligence, which means automating all those routine tasks in order to scale what makes us more human: problem solving, decision making, empathy and imagination. How are you scaling human intelligence in the age of automation?

5. FROM EXPERT TO BEGINNER

I define the beginner's mindset as the gap between what you know and what you want to know. Sadly, most curiosity is educated out of us by the time we've finished college or university. And the ratio of questions you ask drops significantly from when you are a child to when you become an adult. When you have a beginner's mindset, you don't know what can go wrong and are more willing to experiment, which is essential when uncertainty and complexity are high. People who are always in expert mode risk being trapped by their own expertise and becoming blind to their own blindness. Leaders must embrace a beginner's mindset of continual learning and curiosity in order to grab opportunities, break through comfort zones and step into the unknown. Are you ready to step out of your comfort zone and think like a beginner again?

6. FROM CONTROL TO CO-CREATION

I believe leadership is the greatest platform for change but, in many organisations, there's a chronic leadership gap: teams are being over managed and under led. Gallup's latest poll shows that only 15% of employees worldwide are actively engaged at work; productivity is down; stress is up; and 13% of employees have mentally quit the job but haven't physically left the organisation. This is called a 'quit and stay' culture. According to *Management Today*, one in five people would trust a stranger more than their own boss and, according to Edelman's Annual Trust Index, 58% of people do not trust businesses to do the right thing. Something has to change. The best leaders build a 'leaders developing leaders' culture where the leadership style is to inspire and empower, not command and control and where honesty is modelled and decisions are made with integrity.

How often does your team get to play their 'A' game? Old leadership models are badly suited for modern companies which need the agility to move fast. The old model of command and control does not build trust or creativity and these are the new currencies of leadership. Is your leadership style more compliance-led or trust-led?

7. FROM KNOWING TO LEARNING

Author and London Business School Professor Gary Hamel says, 'The most profound business challenge we face today is how to build organisations that can change as fast as change itself.' The ability to learn, unlearn and relearn is one of the most powerful ways to future proof yourself and ensure the rate of change inside an organisation is faster than the rate of change outside. Both leaders and their teams need to cultivate a daily curiosity of asking, observing, exploring and experimenting to avoid falling behind. The last 10 years has shown big companies are dying younger, dropping from an average lifespan of 60 years to less than 15 years. The fact that nearly 9 of every 10 Fortune 500 companies in 1955 are gone, merged or contracted demonstrates that there's been a lot of disruption. This hard trend is set to accelerate as superstar companies such as Square Inc., Tencent and Alibaba choose to disrupt industries adjacent to their own.

The late Harvard Business School professor Clayton Christensen was so eager to encourage questions that he even hung a handmade wooden sign above his office door which said 'anomalies welcome'. What questions do you want to be remembered for? And what could you do to ensure people stop for three minutes everyday to ask new types of questions?

8. FROM TALKING TO ENGAGING

Leaders must now know the difference between communicating and engaging. Most leaders over-communicate but do not engage with their teams. To change the culture and move into new growth areas, you must become a chief storyteller. Everybody must be aligned around the long-term vision and the assumptions about the future that underpin it. But you also have to change the nature of the dialogue, moving away from one about certainty and predictability, and towards one about assumptions and managing risks and setting expectations that change is not something that happens quickly.

When everybody understands the journey, you inspire individuals to contribute something bigger than him or her. It's the difference that makes the difference. How often do messages get lost in translation? Most organisations are drowning in data and clarity is being lost through the hundreds of pointless emails, meetings and 1-2-1s. Pause for a moment and try to estimate the average number of emails that come into your inbox on a daily basis. Ten, fifty? More than 100? In regard to email send per day worldwide, it's about 289 emails sent and received every day and this figure is expected to grow to almost 320 billion daily emails in 2021, according to Statista. Are you in control of email or is email in control of you? Do you email at the expense of face-to-face interaction where trust exchange is at its highest?

9. FROM COMPLIANCE TO COURAGE

Scandals ranging from the #MeToo movement to whistleblowers at the NHS and alleged bullying at the UK Houses of Parliament have shown how pervasive cultures of fear and bullying are in modern-day organisations. Most leaders still reward compliance before courage, hierarchy before empowerment and efficiency before experimentation and, yet, leadership demands that you build psychologically safe and cognitively diverse teams of courageous doers who are able to speak up, learn from failure, challenge old assumptions and move from thinking to doing. Now not taking a risk is a risk. I define culture as what people do when you're not in the room. Do you have a culture of silence or a culture of speak-up? Does your organisation reward doing things right over doing the right things?

10. FROM SLOW TO FAST

Now it's no longer about big or small. It's about fast or slow. According to a recent McKinsey study, 80% of CEOs believe that, in this new reality, their current business model is at risk and only 6% are satisfied with their innovation performance. It used to take, on average, 20 years for a company to reach $1 billion in revenue. Now it can happen within months. The number of 'unicorns', small, fast-growing technology firms with valuations of more than $1 billion, is at record levels. CEOs know that survival requires leading differently and continually finding new ways of doing things that the competition doesn't. Boardrooms are sweating up and down the country as young upstarts force them to completely rethink how they run their companies.

The biggest change that Moore's Law and the internet have caused is the decrease in the amount of time that you need to launch and scale an idea, whether it's Slack achieving a record for the fastest growing unicorn in history or Apple and Microsoft becoming $1 trillion companies. Now speed capital is as important as financial capital. Fearless organisations use speed capital in tandem with financial and human capital. They understand that they are now operating in a high-velocity world where the leader's job is to inspire everyone to deliver more. To do that, you need to develop the next generation of talent that is committed to speed. Do you prioritise speed alongside growth and profitability? How easy is it to make fast decisions without 100% certainty?

ABOUT THIS BOOK

The Chinese have a saying: 'Cure the disease before it happens.' You must start the process of reinvention now and fix problems before they become emergencies. *The 3D Leader* is a proven system that will help you to do great work and excel in a fast, volatile world. Every leader knows that they must step into the unknown to create new things that have not been created before. Many of the ideas in this book come from one of my most popular keynote talks 'How To Thrive In The Age of Disruption'. The talk helps leaders to think bigger, 'see' things that are normally ignored, and find value in what's missing. More than 40,000 people around the world have attended: Fortune 500 leaders to founders of fledgling startups. As a business thinker, speaker and writer, my research constantly takes me around the world. I've met leaders from all walks of life and these encounters have given me a rich insight into what it takes to be a 3D Leader.

When you read *The 3D Leader*, you'll discover more:

- **Leadership purpose.** How alive do you feel at work? Nobody wants to be a 9–5 robot. Human beings are meaning makers. The most ancient part of our brain, the reptilian brain at the back of our head, finds meaning through purpose. In a McKinsey interview with researcher Adam Grant of the University of Pennsylvania's Wharton Business School, Grant explains why purpose matters more than ever: 'If you look at the data, what most employees are looking for in their jobs is a sense of meaning and purpose. And when you look at, in turn, what makes work meaningful, what enables people to feel that their daily lives in organisations are significant – more than anything else it's the belief that "My work makes a difference." That "What I do has some kind of benefit or lasting value to other people."' I think this is something a lot of leaders overlook: talent prizes purpose.

- **Psychological safety.** Can you recall a time when you had something important to say or ask but held back because of fear? According to my own poll of 500 leaders, 87% agreed with the statement that they could recall a time when they held back from speaking up, asking a question or sharing an idea. The ultimate definition of psychological safety is risk, vulnerability and emotional exposure: it's not being afraid to be yourself. It's the belief that one will not be punished or humiliated for speaking up with ideas, questions, concerns or mistakes. In a knowledge economy, where diversity of ideas, experience and cognitive styles are your biggest asset, leaders must build fearless cultures where everybody has a voice and can express it fully. The tragic events of Boeing Max 737 showed that when people are too scared to speak up about their concerns, trust and safety always suffer. If you have knowledge but you can't use it or express it, if you're holding back, then knowledge is lost.

- **Brave work.** The future you create depends on the courage you take today. 3D Leaders shake up the status quo, deal with failure, and make tough decisions fast. Every big 10,000-person company wants to think like a startup: small companies have 'can do' cultures, habits and ways of working that give them an edge over their much larger and cumbersome rivals. Now, more than ever, you must think and act like a disruptor. The recent death of so many iconic companies offers a timely reminder that, if you don't change the status quo, you might just become it. Start before you are ready and know that the best way to disrupt is to challenge long-held assumptions about the world.

And you'll see less:

- **Wasted talent.** Today's organisations waste talent. The terrible state of the workplace reveals painful facts about the absence of a talent focus in today's workplace. Only 33% of employees felt they make optimum use of their talents at work. This means a staggering 67% feel they can't exploit their strengths. This is even more painful when we know that exploiting our strengths is a major driver of motivation. This has consequences. Employees are 15% less likely to quit if they use their strengths daily, and are 8% more productive when they do. My research reveals an important shift – from job descriptions to purpose, talent and mastery. It's a clear differentiator between traditional and fearless organisations. Legacy organisations focus on fixed job descriptions, and linear career paths that move from one description to the next. The 3D Leader focuses less on job descriptions and more on autonomy, talent and mastery.

- **SEP.** This stands for 'somebody else's problem'. It's endemic in many companies and is a productivity killer. You know the characters: blame throwers, energy suckers, silent assassins and chief elusive officers. According to a recent report by Unit4, 20% of people in non-managerial positions have never had contact with their CEO and only 42% have met the CEO in a one-to-one situation. An SEP culture means avoidance: excuses, inertia and lazy back covering. It's the opposite of a culture of ownership. SEP can limit a team, a company and even you, meaning you spend more time on internal turf wars than on building great teams, great products and great talent.

■ **Fear.** Fear is the ultimate innovation killer: fear of failure, fear of change, fear of difference and fear of the unknown can prevent the best-intentioned leader or team from dealing with uncertainty. Let's face it. In most organisations, it's career suicide to fail let alone talk about it. And, while it's currently in fashion to talk about creating a fail fast culture, most organisations are still built to reward compliance rather than experimentation. Fear can cause flight, fight or freeze behaviours and a hasty retreat from your biggest plans. Most of the biggest battles you'll ever fight will be inside your own head between two sides of your brain, risk on the right and fear on the left. Sometimes, you just have to hit the stop button when the voice of fear tries to take over because the left-brain stops innovation in its tracks. A 3D Leader leads more and doubts less – quickly. If you wait for perfection, opportunities are lost forever.

In *The 3D Leader*, you will unlock practical ways to activate the best and boldest version of you and your organisation. I believe that the dimensions of *bold*, *brave* and *beyond* are about pushing you to think differently, breaking out of those little boxes that we get trapped in. It takes guts to change before a crisis forces you to. Now is not the time to stay still. It's time for action. *The 3D Leader* will be the catalyst to launch, scale and accelerate your leadership impact for the long term.

The 3D Leader is organised into six chapters: Introduction: the challenge, Bold, Brave, Beyond, Conclusion: next step actions and The 3D Leader Test. Each chapter will showcase the latest thinking, practical actions and tools to grow each dimension of *bold*, *brave* and *beyond*. Each chapter is useful on its own, but their convergence is the key to igniting the three dimensions to scale the best leader in you. Remove one chapter and the journey slows down. Commit to all of them and rapid reinvention will begin to unfold:

■ **Chapter 1:** 'Hello tomorrow' unlocks the three dimensions of the 3D Leader and argues why this book matters now, which challenges it addresses and how you can expect to take your leadership to the next dimension from reading it.

- **Chapter 2:** the *bold* dimension explains what it means to be a bold leader in more detail and uncovers powerful strategies to think 10x not 10%, take risks and think and act like a startup, no matter what your role or job title.

- **Chapter 3:** the *brave* dimension asks if you speak truth to power and explores how to build a culture of courage where psychological safety and diversity are high.

- **Chapter 4:** the *beyond* dimension explores why the leaders of the future must learn, unlearn and relearn in order to remain resilient and adaptable to the forces of disruption.

- **Chapter 5:** 'next step actions' provides a summary of the three dimensions that make up the 3D Leader and some final practical ways you can take to move from knowing to doing.

- **Chapter 6:** complete the 3D Leader Test to scale the dimensions of bold, brave and beyond and use it to accelerate strengths and flag blind spots.

KEY MESSAGES

- The future arrives faster than ever before. Unhappy customers and employees, broken business models, inertia and legacy cultures mean leaders must update their mindset and their skillset.

- *The 3D Leader* is your blueprint for how to thrive in a world of speed, radical uncertainty and change.

- The leadership dimensions of *bold*, *brave* and *beyond* will help you get uncomfortable with risks and scale the best leader in you.

- What got you to where you are will not get you to where you need to be. *The 3D Leader* will help you close the gap between the leader you are and the leader you want to be.

- Big problems attract big thinkers. 10x thinking is the golden thread that links all 3D Leaders together and stops you from thinking too small.

ACTION

If you do only one thing now, make a stand to bring your best and boldest self to work and commit to scaling the 3D Leader across your whole organisation.

CHAPTER 2

BOLD

The world is not limited by IQ. We are all limited by bravery and creativity.

Astro Teller, Google X

In this chapter you will learn to:

- *thrive in a VUCA world*
- *ask bold questions*
- *unlock the power of 10x thinking*
- *use a beginner's mindset.*

THE NEW LOGIC OF LEADERSHIP

What would it take to build a company that lasts a hundred years or even a thousand years? The history of humanity is a history of disruption:

- 100,000 years ago, we harnessed fire, which led to language.
- 10,000 years ago, we developed agriculture, which led to cities and commerce.
- 5,000 years ago, we invented writing and the wheel, which led to democracy and the nation state.

We've now arrived at a new inflection point in our human history where the convergence of data and technology will completely redefine what it means to be a leader. In a world of AI, algorithms and automation, leaders will need to excel at the art of taking bold leaps into the unknown and doing things they're not sure of.

Winning the present is challenging enough, but the more essential task of leadership is winning the future. The *bold* dimension is the answer. It is defined as 'a daring and decisive leader who thinks bigger and bolder about the future and sees problems and challenges as opportunities'. Bold leaders excel at speed, creativity and decisive action. They are risk takers. It's not the only factor that drives success, but perhaps it is one of the most important in the age of overload. We all face the twin problems of deciding what to do and what to tune out. Imagination enables bold leaders to think of different solutions to a problem and can help you 'cut through the noise' and focus on what really matters. If you want to make an impact, you need to act boldly, especially if you want to thrive in a VUCA world.

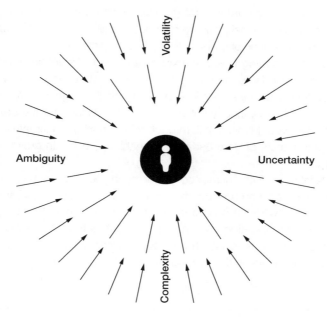

Leading in a VUCA world

VUCA WARRIOR

Today, leaders have to manage VUCA (the US military's acronym for volatility, uncertainty, complexity and ambiguity) on steroids to keep up with a world of hyperchange where the amount of data generated is set to double every 2 years, reaching 40 zettabytes (40 trillion gigabytes), which is the equivalent of 57 times all the grains of sand on Earth by 2027. VUCA is about not just change but the speed of change. Change is a force for learning, discovery and growth. While it can be hard, facing change forces you to learn, move and adapt. Since change is always happening, the questions are: Are you a VUCA warrior? And do you choose to let it happen to you, or do you take an active role in leading change?

Here's a scary question. Why will 80% of the Fortune 1000 be replaced over the next 10 years? First, leaders fall in love with their ego, their thinking, old leadership models and so-called best practices. That means what got you to where you are will not get you to where you want to be; and second, change especially culture change, is really hard. Leading change sounds simple in principle, but in reality is incredibly elusive, with 93% of organisations reporting that they expect significant disruption but do not have the right mindsets, operating models and cultures to turn disruption into opportunity. Business models are going off like yoghurt in the fridge. Obsolete cost bases, legacy cultures and inertia mean that the best way to future proof your leadership is through reinvention and, ultimately, being in a perpetual state of beta because everything is either in growth mode or decay.

On a scale of 1–5 (5 = high), score how much your industry has changed in the last 10 years and how much it will change in the next 10 years. Now ask yourself: how much has your organisation changed? What was the result? If your organisation isn't changing as fast as the world is changing, it's easy to become irrelevant. The new logic of leadership means that leading through disruption is the new norm.

CASE STUDY

I recently received a call from a director at one of the biggest funeral care companies in the world. Her reason for calling was to explore how to scale the bold superpower in an industry that has not changed for thousands of years. From live streaming of funerals to woodland burials, I discovered that even the death industry is being reimagined. After the initial surprise, I felt nothing but respect. I realised that no company or industry is immune from the forces of change any more and that disruption isn't the biggest threat to your organisation's existence. Disruption happens for five reasons:

1. *Unhappy customers.*
2. *Broken business models.*
3. *Obsolete cost bases.*
4. *Legacy cultures.*
5. *Inertia.*

Even to stay the same, everything must change. It requires the bold dimension to initiate and anticipate what your customer needs. The bottom line: you grow bigger by growing bolder.

Questions:

1. Do you see disruption as a threat or an opportunity?

2. Do you have a clear point of view on how to turn disruption into opportunity?

3. Is your organisation changing as fast as your customers are?

4. Do you have safe spaces for employees to create and, more importantly, safe spaces for them to fail?

DAVID VERSUS GOLIATH

The late Pierre Nanterme, former Accenture's CEO, said that, 'digital is the main reason just over half of the companies on the Fortune 500 have disappeared since the year 2000'.

Many companies we know today simply won't exist in the future. Like the story of David versus Goliath, leaders continue to underestimate not just the competition but the battle field. In the ancient fable, Goliath wore heavy armour and held a big sword that was difficult to use. This made him slow and unable to respond quickly to new threats. He got trapped by his experience. He assumed that David would wear the same heavy armour, too. However, David was a disruptor. He had a beginner's mindset and broke the rules and ignored the traditional conventions of hand-to-hand combat. He did not wear heavy armour and did not even bring a sword. In fact, all he carried was a simple slingshot. He was fast, agile and rejected false constraints that disruption is something that just happens to you. Needless to say, he quickly defeated the much bigger and more experienced opponent. Is your organisation a David or a Goliath?

The key to managing the forces of VUCA is understanding that *changes in the operating environment can create new opportunities and result in potentially devastating consequences for those still leading under old models or assumptions*. The demise of travel operator Thomas Cook and the 135-year-old M&S's recent exit from the FTSE100 reflect the shifting sands of VUCA and underscore that leadership means both survival and reinvention. There are several strategies for remaining curious and alert to the forces of VUCA. Companies must walk through the 'valley of death' and overcome significant threats in order to survive: limited resources, risk and little capital. First, you must become an avid learner of leadership.

Learn from good leaders and bad ones throughout your career and read books about leaders whom you admire in history. The deep insights and lessons you can assimilate are priceless. Next, find a mentor and don't just settle for one. Aim for multiple mentors with different backgrounds whom you can tap for ideas or advice. Most of all, get into the game – this means grab opportunities, break through comfort zones and take the risk.

THE OBSTACLE IS THE WAY

The Roman Emperor Marcus Aurelius wrote: 'Our actions may be impeded . . . but there can be no impeding our intentions or our dispositions. Because we can accommodate and adapt. The mind adapts and converts to its own purposes the obstacle to our acting.'

All of the major developments of modern civilisation have depended on a person's, or group of people's, ability to discover possible futures and to be bold enough to dream and go where no one has gone before. It is about taking a leap of faith and trusting that, when the moment comes, you are able to keep up the practice, stand behind the vision and push through the obstacles.

A new study published in the *Journal of Personality and Social Psychology*, by researcher Janina Marguc at the University of Amsterdam, supports this hypothesis that obstacles induce bold thinking:

'Daily life is full of obstacles: a construction site blocking the usual road to work, a colleague's background chatter interfering with one's ability to concentrate, a newborn child hindering parents in completing their daily routines, or a lack of resources standing in the way of realizing an ambitious plan.

How do people cognitively respond to such obstacles? How do the ways in which they perceive and process information from their environment change when an obstacle interferes with what they want to accomplish? In the present research, we aim to shed light on these questions by investigating the impact of obstacles on global versus local processing. We propose that unless people are inclined to disengage prematurely from ongoing activities, obstacles will prompt them to step back and adopt a more global, Gestalt-like processing style that allows them to look at the "big picture" and conceptually integrate seemingly unrelated pieces of information.'

It turns out that overcoming obstacles provides an unexpected motivational boost, pushing you to deliver more than is expected. The stakes are higher but so are the rewards. An illustration of this is the story of Drew Houston, CEO of the startup file-sharing company Dropbox. He came up with the idea for the company after he forgot his flash drive and could not work on a long bus ride from Boston to New York.

Adversity is a natural part of the leadership journey. Every leader I have met, from Mary Barra at General Motors to Ginni Rometty at IBM, has had to show courage in the face of adversity, from trade wars to navigating global pandemics. At some point, you will open the door and face your own obstacle. It could be finding the strength to tackle a failure or bouncing back from a personal tragedy or setback. Mine came when I was seven years old – a driver sped out of control, mounted a curb and crashed into a shop where my family and I were standing. We nearly lost our lives. Ever since that day, I've understood that part of the power of bold lies in its hope-inducing nature. It's the spark plug of all action and it's the split moment to remember you always have a choice either to accept defeat or push past barriers and overcome fear.

CASE STUDY

Every leader has their own demons to face, courage to find and decisions to make. Anne Boden is the founder of Starling Bank that is reinventing how we do our banking and is a leader who has grown bolder not by avoiding fear but by facing it. Here are three of the biggest fears leaders must overcome and, in so doing, grow better and bolder along the way.

1. *Fear of failure. This happens when you focus more on failure than success. It's important to flip this to: failure is one half of success. Stop worrying about the rate of failure because, as long as those failures are cheap, you can afford a lot of them. As the saying goes, 'fail fast, fail cheap and move on'. To fail intelligently, you need to focus on brave actions such as exploring, experimenting and innovating:*

   ■ *Hedge your bets.*

   ■ *Test and learn.*

   ■ *Cheap, simple experiment.*

▶

2. *Fear of difference.* *This means that often we strive to fit in and, along the way, lose who we are and what we stand for. The best way to overcome fear of difference is to focus on making it safe for others to fully express themselves:*

   - *Remember, differences are good.*

   - *Your differences are a superpower.*

   - *Celebrate differences.*

3. *Fear of change.* *Let's face it, many leaders suffer from change fatigue and the easiest thing to do is just react to change not be the change. A good way to overcome fear of change is to remember that change means renewal, learning and growth. Oliver Sacks wrote 'change means being in a state of becoming throughout our lives'. What do we wish to become?*

   - *Don't focus on change. Focus on renewal.*

   - *Remember you're either changing or stagnating.*

   - *Change means protecting what's good, letting go of what's bad and starting something new.*

Questions:

1. How could you help your teams embrace change and deal with adversity?
2. What steps are you taking to build a team of courageous doers and initiative takers?
3. Do you use setbacks and obstacles as sources of learning and discovery?

ASK BOLD QUESTIONS

Waves of disruption are creating an atmosphere where safety looks like the right option but it never is. Evolution comes before survival only in the dictionary. We are creatures of reason, programmed to preserve energy and maintain equilibrium. The bold dimension will help you bear the initial discomfort and reap the ultimate rewards. It is the ability to imagine the future, take extraordinary action and stay determined when all the odds are against us. One of its underlying premises is that there is more strength to us than meets the eye. It is our ability to take action against impossible odds, transform barriers into frontiers, exceed ourselves, and see beyond the limitations of the present moment. One could define it as the second wind of mental endurance or the sixth gear of tenacity. It's a force that allows you to push through the unimaginable and it starts with asking bold questions.

WHAT QUESTIONS DO YOU WANT TO BE REMEMBERED FOR?

In organisations, sometimes the most obvious questions don't get asked. Next time you are in a meeting or a board meeting, ask yourself: what questions do I want to be remembered for? When you're leading at the edge of uncertainty, questions matter more than answers.

CASE STUDY

The Chinese coffee company Luckin Coffee did not exist three years ago and, yet, today is already set to take over Starbucks in China. It's opening a new store every four hours in China, going from just 9 stores to over 2,000 in 1 year. You have to order by app and can watch a live stream of your coffee being made while you wait. Luckin focuses on scale and speed not just profit, although it's already valued at $2.2 billion. To scale fast, Luckin Coffee leaders ask bold questions across every part of the leadership value chain from talent and metrics to learning and growth:

1. *Rate of learning – are we learning, exploring and experimenting?*
2. *Resilience – is our business model adaptable and resilient in the face of accelerating change?*
3. *Customer obsession – are we committed to building a frictionless world for our customers?*
4. *Talent – do we have a talent-first strategy to retain and grow our human advantage?*
5. *Technology-led – are we investing in technology to automate and elevate the customer experience on the outside and the people experience on the inside?*

Questions:

1. What's the boldest question you've asked of your team?
2. How could you use new types of questions to unlock new ways of seeing the world?
3. How do you create a culture that is more focused on asking the right question than pleasing the right people?

WE ARE BLIND TO OUR OWN BLINDNESS

What stops you from asking the biggest questions and challenging the status quo? In most organisations, leaders are on autopilot, asking the same questions every day and getting the same answers. Bold questions can help you find new solutions to old problems and new solutions to new problems. As everybody will have access to the information, asking bold questions will matter more than ever. Ask: Why? Why Not? How? What if? What if not? What else? Who? When? By When? They can help you close the gap between what you know and what you want to know and shake up old ways of seeing the world. Here are 25 bold questions to blow up old mindsets and assumptions and focus on new ways of thinking.

BOLD QUESTIONS FOR BOLD ANSWERS

Questions to win the future

1. What will it take to win in the future?
2. How do you break out of old patterns of thinking?
3. How do you change before a crisis forces you to?
4. What must we unlearn?
5. Which old mindsets, assumptions and operating models must we let go of?

Questions to collaborate better

1. Are we a group or a team?
2. Do we emphasise collective or individual goals?
3. Do we hire originals with different viewpoints and expertise?

4. Do we have a speak up culture or a culture of silence?

5. Do we celebrate collaboration efforts in meaningful ways?

Questions to inspire and empower

1. Do we set teams up for success by removing obstacles and providing support?

2. Do we encourage an 'owner' mentality or play the blame game?

3. Are teams empowered to solve problems without asking for permission?

4. Is everyone empowered to fight complexity with simplicity?

5. Do teams have the tools to achieve their full potential?

Questions to learn and experiment

1. Do we plan for different scenarios and alternative outcomes?

2. Do we constantly ask ourselves what we don't know and how we can learn more?

3. Do we reward teams for learning, experimenting and intelligent failure?

4. Do we design simple experiments to test assumptions about an idea?

5. Do we spend enough time with our customers to understand the job that needs to be done?

Questions to show courage

1. Do we ask the bravest questions of each other?

2. Are we perpetually paranoid about the future?

3. Do we understand how to turn disruptors into opportunities?

4. Do we speak up and disagree about issues that matter?

5. Do we show courage in our daily work?

The future you create depends on the questions you dare to ask today. All of the great advancements of leadership are based on our ability to expand our psychological horizon, take a step into the unknown and make a path where there is none. What this means is that we have to ask new questions in order to see around corners and peek into the future. Now more, perhaps, than ever, we need the ability to imagine a new future and take action. Remaining complacent by asking the same questions will stall progress, and it's those with the bold questions who can lead the quest for success.

CASE STUDY

In his best-selling book Behind the Cloud: The untold story of how salesforce.com went from idea to billion-dollar company—and revolutionized an industry, *CEO Marc Benioff reveals what he learned from Oracle legend Larry Ellison. He writes: 'Always have a vision. Be passionate. Act confident, even when you're not.' Done well, this is a catalyst for action. Use the bold questions below to scale high performance across the whole leadership value chain.*

Leadership purpose:

1. Why do you do what you do?
2. Complete the sentence: My leadership purpose is _____.
3. Do you live it daily?
4. Imagine five years ahead and describe your ultimate vision for yourself and your organisation.
5. How often do you get to do what you do best every day?
6. How do you achieve meaning and impact in your role?
7. How do you put your leadership purpose to work more?

Values:

1. What is vital to you?
2. What makes someone a real hero?
3. What makes you happy?
4. Which leaders do you admire and why?
5. What principles do you choose to lead by?
6. When you fall or have a setback, how do you pick yourself up?

Vision:

1. What do you like most about the vision?
2. Describe the vision in one sentence.

3. How can you support the vision?

4. How well are you performing against the vision?

Culture:

1. Describe your culture in one word.

2. What do you value most?

3. Do we have a culture by design or by accident?

4. How do you scale culture and sustain it?

5. What kind of people are you hiring?

6. What talent do you attract?

7. What makes someone a role model?

8. Which cultures do you admire and why?

9. What do you like most about your culture?

10. How will I sustain all of the above?

BOLD LEADERS TAKE BOLD RISKS

Silicon Valley is 1,500 square miles of the most fertile ground on the planet and a giant launch pad for some of the world's most well-known start-ups. Cisco Systems, Intel, eBay and Hewlett-Packard are just some of the companies that have made it their home. What makes this area unique is a combination of access to capital, talent and innovation. In the Bay area alone, more than 90% of companies have an innovation strategy supported by their top team. What's telling is, irrespective of size, they cultivate a belief system that with a 10x mindset anything is possible. Paul Graham at the incubator Y Combinator says: 'Live in the future, then build what's missing.' Success is no longer about being big or small. Now fast eats slow. It's about blitz scaling, which means growing 10x faster than the norm. The average time it used to take to reach a valuation of $1 billion or more was 20 years for a typical Fortune 500 company but, today, companies such as Xiaomi, Tesla and Snapchat are reaching this unicorn status in less than two years and are aiming to become decacorns ($10 billion) and hectocorns ($100 billion). The 3D Leader models a Silicon Valley mindset: it thinks big, acts small and moves fast.

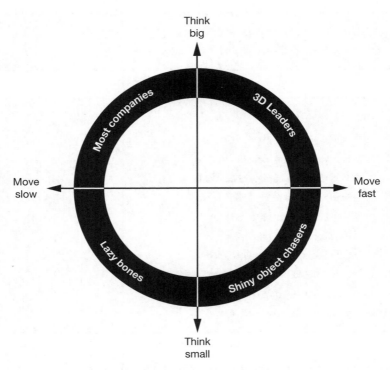

Silicon Valley mindset

WHAT YOU DO IS WHO YOU ARE

How do you prepare a culture to solve a problem? Leaders create culture, culture drives behaviour and behaviour produces results. I define culture as what your employees do when you're not in the room. One of the key insights from Zen philosophy is that a culture is not a set of beliefs, it's a set of actions. In Silicon Valley, companies have a startup culture, whether they are big or small, and are known for their agile decision making, rapid prototyping and flat structures. In Silicon Valley, there is a saying that not taking a risk is a risk. A bold journey is inherently risky. Changes are made quickly and then adjusted for optimisation, and failure is not a badge of shame, it's a badge of honour. Leaders radiate optimism and genuinely care about what you're doing. I call it passionate curiosity. Instead of asking, 'What do you do?' they'll ask: 'How can I help and who do you know?' There's a freedom to be yourself: nobody is waiting for approval or permission. It's impossible not to feel hugely invigorated by the energy, ideas and sheer determination to make things happen. This type of environment can have a big impact on the way you think about risk taking, perhaps unlike anywhere else on the planet.

Reed Hastings at Netflix is a good example of a leader who uses a Silicon Valley startup culture to gain an unfair competitive advantage. Not only has he changed his business model at least three times – DVD mail delivery, film streaming and film production – he understands that your company's culture can be either a strategic asset or a potential liability. At Netflix, there are five talent tenets to attract, recruit and retain A+ talent. They are:

1. Hire, reward and tolerate only fully formed adults.
2. Tell the truth about performance.
3. Managers own the job of creating great teams.
4. Leaders own the job of creating the company culture.
5. Good talent managers think like businesspeople and innovators first, and like HR people last.

CASE STUDY

At Booking.com, innovation means constant risk taking. Unlike most organisations, Booking.com embraces a culture where testing, experimentation and learning from failure are essential. Anybody can launch an experiment at Booking.com where you don't need to ask for permission and anybody can also kill an experiment that somebody else has launched. Failure is regarded as the status quo so, if 9 out 10 things fail, it's essential to build a learn fast, move fast culture.

Big change starts small

It's not necessarily about big change but more about high speed iteration whereby small changes can lead to huge performance changes.

How do you scale intelligent failure in your organisation where everybody owns the future of the company? Booking.com removes the biggest barriers to innovation by giving everybody the tools to experiment, ask questions and even criticise. At any one time, there are over 1,000 iterations of the Booking.com website, which results in millions of variations that are used for continuous learning and improvement.

▶

The question Booking.com leaders ask every day is: How am I building small, empowered agile teams?

Do more:

- *autonomy*
- *context*
- *purpose*
- *trust*
- *delegation*
- *coaching and feedback.*

Do less:

- *command and control*
- *hierarchy*
- *controlling everything*
- *reacting*
- *assuming worst intentions*
- *unproductive meetings.*

What's the result of Booking.com's do more, do less approach? One of the world's fastest growth travel companies with over 2 million room bookings per night and over 400 million visits per month.

Questions:

1. How do you build purpose and autonomy into the roles of your team?
2. To empower others, do you focus on context more than control?
3. Do you have a team of truth tellers? If not, why?

BOLD LEADERSHIP

I believe every leader should place bold leadership at the heart of its culture. I asked more than 1,000 leaders working in companies how they rated the bold dimension at work. Only three out of ten respondents agreed that bold was a strength in their organisation.

The three biggest obstacles leaders must overcome in order to unlock the bold leadership are:

1. **Organisational barriers.** Status quo mindset, bureaucracy and fear of failure are some of the biggest innovation killers. Fear is the enemy of innovation: fear of judgement, fear of the unknown and fear of losing your job can prevent the best-intentioned leader or team from changing. To encourage innovation, a leader must incentivise risk taking and put the bold dimension at the heart of its culture. How are you shaping the bold dimension for your team?

2. **Cognitive barriers.** The demands on leaders' time make it hard for the brain to look ahead and think clearly. Thanks to unhealthy eating and sleeping habits, our brains are rarely in peak condition. Information overload, old habits and sloppy thinking can literally stop innovation in its tracks. I worked with one forward-thinking organisation that held 'walk and talk' meetings and met in different locations every week to stay upbeat. The best leaders let their minds wander. Take a brain break: go for a walk and get some fresh air. This is often where great ideas lie dormant. How do you ensure your brain is in peak condition?

3. **Schlep blindness.** There are great ideas lying around unexploited right under our noses. One reason we don't see them is a phenomenon I call *schlep blindness*. *Schlep* was originally a Yiddish word but has passed into general use in the USA. It means a tedious, unpleasant task. Leaders are often guilty of schlep blindness, adopting avoidance behaviours, such as procrastination or making excuses, which ensures that a potential idea dies early. The best strategy is to just dive right in. Don't wait. Don't overthink and, when you hit a wall, take a break or move into a new environment. To overcome schlep blindness, write down your fears and bounce ideas around with the team. Ideas usually go through a series of stages from 'that's a bad idea' to 'that's a good idea' and then, finally, 'that's my idea'. Ideas can be obvious but hard, easy and overcrowded, or not obvious but hard. Be open to hidden insights: prototype ideas quickly until they make sense and remember most good ideas start as bad ideas. Are you aware of your own blind spots? What could you do to be more open to hidden insights?

Most leaders today are trying to do the same things: help their organisations become more agile, more innovative and more customer-centric. If leaders all do the same things and don't embrace the bold dimension, their very existence becomes threatened. Who would have predicted that the world's most valuable company 10 years ago, General Electric, would lose 90% of its market value today, or car manufacturer Volkswagen would find itself at the centre of a public relations disaster and that the once mighty smartphone manufacturer BlackBerry would lose its way? It's no accident that Silicon Valley is a household name today all around the world. Its herculean rise is, in large part, due to 10x thinking from the 'father of Silicon Valley', Frederick Terman to, in more recent times, Apple's Steve Jobs and Google's Larry Page and Sergey Brin. These leaders have thrown out the rulebook on leadership: the bold dimension demands you to rethink assumptions about what is possible.

BREAK THE RULES

Tech is reshaping industries faster than ever before but leaders are struggling to respond to these changes. Competitive lines are being redrawn and the idea of companies staying in their own lane has gone away. Threats come from unexpected places: Amex and Visa now compete with Alibaba and Daimler must contend with insurgents such as Uber and Amazon. The bold dimension requires leaders to break out of old mindsets and assumptions about what they believe to be true. When was the last time you challenged a bias or changed a long-held assumption? Now the dominant logic we held for decades has been disproved in the last decade:

1. No one will get a ride in a stranger's car (Uber).
2. No one will rent their homes to strangers (Airbnb).
3. Most companies will not store their critical data in the cloud (Amazon AWS).
4. No one will order food online (Deliveroo).

The bold dimension is about reimagining the future and asking, if we started again today, what would be different? Astro Teller is a British entrepreneur, scientist and thinker who is widely credited as one of the pioneers of moonshot thinking. He heads up Google X, a futuristic lab responsible for hyper-ambitious projects such as Project Loon, a balloon-powered Wi-Fi network, and the infamous Google self-driving car, Waymo. According to legend, his business card describes him as 'Captain of Moon Shots'. In an interview with *Wired* magazine, Teller explains the power of bold thinking: Perspective shifting from ten per cent better to ten times better is what it's all about when it comes to thinking big at Google. This means three things: identify huge problems, discover radical solutions and use breakthrough technology. Most leaders simply think too small and get trapped by their own limited perspectives about the world. Ten times better is about replacing fears and limits with questions. If you had to make a car that goes 100 miles a gallon, you can just apply incremental thinking and optimise the engine to reach 100 miles per gallon. But if I challenge you to cast aside your existing assumptions about car engines and tell you that it has to run on a gallon of gas for 500 miles, you will have to re-think everything which counter-intuitively increases your chances of shifting from ten per cent better to ten times better. What could you do to unblock the power of moonshots in your own organisation?

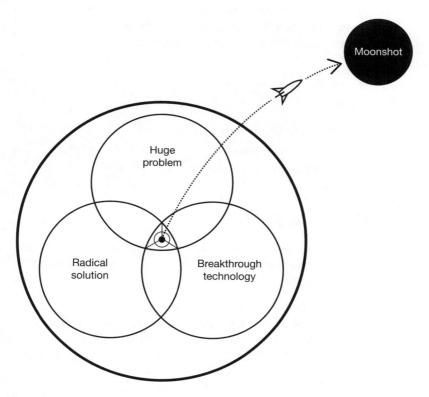

What's your moonshot?

CASE STUDY

Leaders should always be searching for 10x ways of working. How much time a year do you spend on scheduling and rescheduling meetings? This is the burning question Dennis Mortensen, the founder of x.ai, a New York startup, asked himself when one year he realised that he was spending 20% of his week on scheduling and rescheduling meetings. Every year, organisations waste more than £37 billion on bad meetings. A slide poll I conducted with 1,000 leaders showed that 70% of employees rated their last three meetings as below expectations. Do your meetings exceed, meet or fall behind on expectations? x.ai is a technology company whose mission is to make meeting scheduling obsolete. Driven by artificial intelligence and human empathy, it has developed a virtual assistant Amy and her male counterpart Andrew Ingram (their initials are AI). Amy and Andrew Ingram have one job only: to arrange meetings. Consider how much time and energy you and your team could get back by automating the most repetitive and soul-sucking parts of your job.

Questions:

1. Are your meetings exceeding, meeting or falling behind on expectations?
2. How could you 10x your meetings to energise and empower your team?
3. If meetings really matter, are you measuring them?

THINK 10X, NOT 10%

In our lifetime, technology has advanced at an extraordinary rate (the first web browser was invented only in 1994 and the first iPhone in 2007). Consider these facts:

1. It took the telephone 75 years to reach 100 million users and WhatsApp just 7 years to reach 1 billion users. WhatsApp achieved this mind-blowing scale with fewer than 50 staff and sold it to Facebook for more than $19 billion. To put that deal in perspective, at the time of purchase, the hotel chain Marriott International had over 120,000 staff and a market cap of $15.4 billion.

2. Slack Technologies, Inc., the popular workplace app which stands for Searchable Log of All Conversation and Knowledge, reached a

$1 billion valuation within just 8 months of its launch in 2013 and is growing by as much as 7% a week, adding thousands of new users every hour. Today, it's valued at over $7 billion, with over 8 million active users a day and clients ranging from Capital One and eBay to IBM.

3. It used to cost around $20 for a CD album of your favourite artist with up to 12 songs for your listening pleasure. Today, you can access a music library of over 100 million artists for less than the cost of a Starbucks coffee.

4. The first human genome took $2.7 billion and almost 15 years to complete. Now, genome sequencing and analysis cost around $1,400 and can be done by startups, such as 23andMe, in just a few days. In the near future, contact lenses that can monitor glucose levels, 3D printed body parts and digestible cameras the size of a piece of grain will be the norm.

A moonshot is a 10x goal that stops you from thinking too small and in incremental ways. Let's face it, most leaders focus on 10% improvements rather than thinking what others aren't thinking and doing what others aren't doing. Imagine that you have a customer process that takes 10 days to complete. A 10% improvement might save a day of time but a 10x goal might mean you reduce the process time to one day or even one hour. A 10x goal forces you to think bigger and bolder so you approach the problem more creatively by completely rethinking what is possible from the bottom up. We tend to associate 10x just with new ideas, but it's possible to apply it to anything in your organisation, from improving culture to how you scale more rapidly. Even if you achieve only 60% of a 10x goal, you will have grown your team and your business, and probably learned some important things about yourself along the way. I have come to the conclusion that you can 10x any part of your leadership role when you choose the right mindset. For example, tech company Alibaba has a 10x goal to build a technology stack ecosystem that handles a million transactions per second for 2 billion people, compared to Visa that handles about 2,000 transactions per second.

Here are seven 10x principles that you can use to think 10x, whether you're leading a global organisation trapped in by legacy or looking to scale a startup.

To unlock the power of 10x for yourself, your team and organisation, ask how do we:

- scale 10x amid increasing customer choice and expectations?
- respond 10x faster to external trends, anomalies and risks?
- reduce 10x rules, processes and protocols?
- build a 10x culture where people bring their best selves to work?
- execute 10x faster on decisions?
- increase 10x our rate of learning?
- reduce 10x the pain points and friction facing our customers?

CASE STUDY

Instagram co-founders Kevin Systrom and Mike Krieger use the 10x principles to scale big by focusing on scale, focus and execution. The result? 30 million users in 18 months and 1 billion active users accessing the platform today. 10x boils down to three things: launching a bold purpose, scaling rapidly and leading by the principle that the best way to know is to do. Sometimes, your 10x goals need to be renewed or even replaced, and that's OK. There will be times when you run off course or even lose your way. Don't become a prisoner to a process that no longer serves you or, worse, is hurting you or holding you back.

Questions:

1. Are you a prisoner to outdated rules, processes and protocols?
2. Are you fighting complexity with complexity? Or fighting complexity with simplicity?
3. What are you doing to eliminate or automate the most soul-sucking parts of your job and your teams' jobs?

HELPING ELEPHANTS TO DO BALLET

Samsung Electronics is an elephant that does ballet. It's also the world's largest smartphone and television manufacturer and holds prominent market positions in a number of industries from memory chips to tablet computers. It has a prestigious heritage – it was founded in 1938 – but, conversely, it has been bold enough to disrupt itself faster in order to stay ahead of the competition. Change is part of the DNA of everything it does and, for this reason, the company continues to grow, despite competition from startups as well as behemoths such as Apple, Microsoft and Google. At Samsung, one of their values is to change everything except their partners and kids.

SNCF, France's national state-owned railway company, is another example of a big company that has become a disruptor. Founded in 1938, it realised it was rapidly losing market share to the popular long-distance carpooling service BlaBlaCar. In order to lure people back and have them experience what it's like to take an intercity train, they launched a €79/ month unlimited subscription service for students. This move turned out to be hugely successful, with about 100,000 students signing up within months. It also meant that an 80-something government-owned corporate was taking back market share from a disruptive startup like BlaBlaCar. The incumbent had become the disruptor.

Every big 50,000-person company understands the value in transforming to agile, adaptive and responsive enterprises because they already have the other intangibles in place, such as a strong brand: small companies have 'can do' cultures, habits and ways of working that give them an edge over their much larger and cumbersome rivals. Now, more than ever, you must think and act like a disruptor. The recent death of so many iconic companies offers a timely reminder that protecting the status quo is the fastest route to obsolescence.

There are three major death traps that you must avoid in order to remain viable:

- **Success trap.** Here's an irony. The thing that made your company successful is the very thing that can destroy you. What if Blockbuster had been able to leave late fees behind or Kraft Heinz had reinvented its brands? The success paradox is the strange phenomenon whereby leaders are busy protecting the golden goose with fear-based, micro improvements while new competitors are busy changing the world. Leaders forget, at their peril, that the risk of staying the same is always greater than the risk of innovation.

- **Ego trap.** Daniel Kahneman, psychologist, says: 'We are blind to our own blindness.' When the first iPhone was launched in 2007, Microsoft's Steve Ballmer said that 'nobody would pay $800 for a mobile with no keyboard' and, when asked about Google, he said: 'It's not a company but a house of falling cards.' Since then, Apple has sold 1.2 billion iPhones. Another time, I remember having dinner with some Nokia executives in Helsinki and the first thing they did was show me their new iPhones. I thought to myself, this isn't a good sign of things to come.

- **Legacy trap.** Big established incumbents can easily get stuck in the legacy trap. They can become risk averse and tend to become too comfortable doing the same thing, just making incremental change rather than continuous transformation. Some very successful organisations are also very complex, drowning in rules, risk controls and compliance. One such example is HSBC, known in some circles as 'How Simple Becomes Complicated'. A hugely successful bank with a proud history of banking spanning over 150 years, it has recently reduced the number of job titles from over 40,000 to fewer than 20,000. With this level of complexity, the number of rules, protocols and processes can force any large company to spend more time fighting complexity than on its customers. So, what's the best way to avoid these existential traps? It starts and finishes with continuous reinvention.

Haier (pronounced Higher) is the world's largest appliance maker on a mission to avoid becoming a prisoner of its own success. Led by CEO Zhang Ruimin, he has spent the last 30 years reinventing the company into a customer-first organisation that continually reinvents itself as it expands around the world. The world is changing, even if we are not. Embracing change, either by changing oneself or fostering change in the company, is a unique part of Haier's DNA and must be valued. One of Zhang's most important leadership principles is an 'owner mentality' and this starts with building the right culture that is the mindsets, values and behaviours practised in that organisation. Most organisations can be defined by one of five cultures.

FIVE COMPANY CULTURES

1. **HiPPO culture:** a culture where hierarchical decision making and boss leadership is the norm.
2. **Bureaucratic culture:** a culture that prioritises excess bureaucracy: rules, processes and protocols.
3. **Hero culture:** a culture that focuses on a small pool of star performers at the expense of everybody else.
4. **Lazy culture:** a culture where inertia, excuses and mediocrity is the norm.
5. **Owner culture:** a culture where everyone thinks like an owner and pursues a relentless focus on excellence.

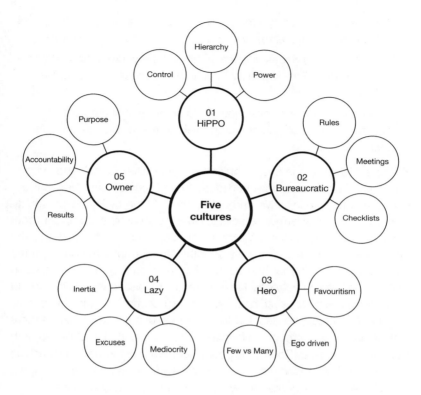

Five company cultures

Zhang says, 'As a company gets bigger, there is usually stricter control on its employees and less room for them to take ownership of their work. This is a challenge for both Chinese companies and companies all across the world.'

Zhang decided to build an owner culture to transform the organisation in seven distinct ways:

1. Context, not control, by helping everybody to think and act like an owner.

2. Hierarchy to self-managing teams in order to build internal competition, speed and agility.

3. Efficiency to empowerment where teams have the freedom to generate their own ideas and solutions to customer needs.

4. Management to entrepreneurs by giving everybody a share of the resulting profits.

5. Complexity to simplicity. Complexity increases dependency. When you reduce complexity, teams are more empowered and more effective.

6. Disruption and changes happen at the periphery, like snow melts at the edges, therefore spend more time at the edges and out of the building.

7. Transformation is everyone's job. Build an army of champions – identify, recruit, motivate and empower them and give them flat, fast operating structure.

Zhang explains: 'In the past, employees would listen to their supervisors, but today they are responsible directly to their customers. We want our employees to take initiative and create value.' One of Zhang's favourite stories is how a rural farmer called in to Haier's call centre to complain about dirt in the washing machine. When a Haier engineer met the customer, he discovered the dirt wasn't from the clothes the farmer wore but from the harvest itself. The farmer had been using the washing machine to wash both his clothes and potatoes. Now, for most organisations, the story would have ended there. However, because the engineer had complete autonomy to think for himself, he decided to run an experiment to validate if there was an unmet customer need for washing machines that could wash both clothes and potatoes. Today, the upgraded version of the washing machine has helped Haier become the leading home appliance maker in the world, with global revenue increasing by 20% year-on-year to $40 billion.

Questions:

1. Which company culture is your organisation: HiPPO, Heroic, Rules, Excuse or Owner?

2. Do you have a culture that rewards customer obsession, autonomy and high-speed decision making?

3. Does your team have the freedom to solve any problem that may occur?

4. Are your leaders role-modelling the cultural values that you want?

CASE STUDY

How do you turn around the legacy culture of a 130,000-person company? Microsoft CEO Satya Nadella is one of the most bold leaders on the planet. Today, it will be seven years since Nadella was announced as Microsoft's Chief

Executive. Since taking charge, he has turned Microsoft's fortunes around, making it the most valuable company in the world for the first time since 2002. Nadella understands that success doesn't happen overnight. Rather, you must think longterm, plant seeds for the future and start reinventing the core business today while building growth engines for tomorrow. This means rethinking everything in your business from becoming an AI-first company to scaling a learning, exploring and experimenting culture. One of Nadella's first bold moves was to change the mission from the archaic-sounding 'a computer on every desk in every home' to the much more customer-focused aim of helping every individual and business to be more productive. Another bold move was to scale a 'leaders developing leaders' mindset, where people are 1. Willing to trust and 2. Willing to change.

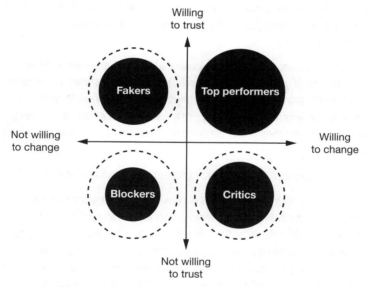

Willing to trust

Bold traits at Microsoft

1. *Speed.*

2. *Data-driven decision making.*

3. *Commitment from the top.*

4. *Entrepreneurial culture.*

5. *Relentless focus on customers.*

6. *Willing to trust and willing to change.*

Nadella quotes philosopher Friedrich Nietzsche, telling colleagues that Microsoft must have 'courage in the face of reality'. Nadella asks five bold questions:

1. **Innovation:** how successful is the business at launching new growth engines? For example, Microsoft acquired social networking site LinkedIn for $26 billion.

2. **Core:** how adaptable and resilient are we at turning disruptors into opportunities and updating the core for the future?

3. **Results:** can we show strong financials and market performance?

4. **Growth mindset:** do we have a growth mindset (learner) or a fixed mindset (knower)?

5. **Human scale:** are we scaling what makes us human more than machines? For example, learning, empathy, imagination, problem solving and creativity.

A 10x culture means moving from a know-it-all mindset to a learn-it-all one. One of your most urgent leadership priorities is to create a shared 10x mindset for the organisation and to remove mental or emotional barriers to change including fear, uncertainty and doubt (FUD). Nadella uses a formula for scaling 10x and mobilising everyone in the company to own the vision. Now you have a movement.

Leadership = (Direction + Alignment) × Execution at speed

Have alignment talks to keep everyone focused on executing top priorities quickly. This means delegating, clarifying, allocating resources and, most importantly, celebrating individual and team success. Be ready to 10x all your internal processes including your annual performance review and the way people prioritise their work. Teams are encouraged to focus on passion projects and think of Microsoft not as a 45-year-old company but as a challenger organisation with day one in its DNA. This seemingly counterintuitive approach acknowledges that the use of defensive language can result in outdated mental models that stop you from reinventing at speed and scale. Nadella knows that now, more than ever, you must use the bold dimension to stay ahead of the curve. The results? Microsoft's Azure platform alone is a $30 billion area of new growth for Microsoft and Nadella is one of the most admired leaders for turning around its fortunes.

THINK LIKE JEFF BEZOS

One of the best ways to understand business is to study biology. Starting with the head, if you think about it, Google is like God. Every day, there are over 5 billion searches on Google, which translates to over 2 trillion searches a year. Think of a coach or a parent and it doesn't take much imagination to know that Google knows more about you than you probably know about yourself. Next, let's move down to the heart that, for Facebook, is a strategy I call 'love at scale'. Despite bad press in the media, it still can boast over 2 billion daily users and is like a giant lab for hacking humans. The next part of the body is the stomach and this is where Amazon rules because, in one word, its strategy is 'more'. Think about how much stuff you have at home that you don't really need and you'll begin to understand why the Amazonification of the world is unstoppable. If you had invested just $100 in Amazon's IPO in 1997, you would have received 5 shares. What is beyond impressive is that investment would yield an increase of more than 120,000% on the initial $100 investment. Now the best part is that Amazon has a Benjamin Button quality to its business model. Think about it. Most business models age with time and, eventually, become obsolete. For Amazon, it's the opposite. Every time you buy from Amazon's platform, its algorithms learn more about you and therefore get smarter and better.

So how do you think like Jeff Bezos?

DAY 1 THINKING

For Jeff Bezos at Amazon, the job of the leader, first and foremost, is to recruit people who are willing to think beyond today. This means there are basically two types of thinking for most leaders – Day 1 or Day 2.

Day 1

Day 1 thinking is a 'customer-first' mindset, which takes as its starting point an obsessive focus on a customer's needs and then works backwards to figure out how to innovate to best meet those needs by using the best talent and technology:

- **Customer obsession:** start every process with the customer and work backwards.
- **Human-led:** the answer to digital is human first.
- **Long-term thinking:** be stubborn on vision and flexible on details.
- **A failure pioneer:** be willing to put the errors in to succeed.
- **Purpose-driven:** purpose is your source code for success.
- **Operationally nimble:** think and act like a startup.
- **Built for speed:** speed capital is as important as financial capital.

Day 1 is, ultimately, a beginner's mindset. I define beginner's mindset as set aside status quo to challenge assumptions and explore new possibilities. Uncertain times call for courage. Don't get frightened by not knowing things. It's OK to have approximate answers and different degrees of certainty about different things. Bezos leads by this principle. As a leader, you can get trapped by your own expertise. When you're an expert, you're more likely to think of the hundreds of ways it can go wrong and have less tolerance for learning, exploring and experimenting. The Japanese call this beginner's state *shoshin* and it is in direct contrast to the expert mind. Being present in the moment, there are many possibilities but, in the expert's, there are few. Don't get frightened by not knowing things. It's OK to have approximate answers and different degrees of certainty about different things – in fact, this is what it means to be human.

When you are Day 1, you make the decision that every day will be a new day where experimenting, inventing and innovating is the norm. A Day 1 company empowers everybody to own their decisions and give them multiple paths to yes. In a VUCA world, where speed capital is as important as financial capital, waiting for 100% certainty before making a decision is not just too slow but results in missing out on game-changing opportunities. Amazon uses two kinds of decision making. Type 1 decisions are not reversible, and you have to be very careful making them. Type 2 decisions are like walking through a door – if you don't like the decision, you can always go back.

CASE STUDY

Tesla is a Day 1 company that follows five principles:

1. *Ask better questions for better outcomes.*
2. *Unleash the power of storytelling.*
3. *To change the culture, change the structure, rewards and incentives.*
4. *Failure and invention are inseparable twins.*
5. *Behind every decision is a customer.*

For example, it holds regular meetings with talk of the new, bold and experimental. It may be a quarterly operations review or exploring the huge potential of a 3D printing facility. For leaders, it sends a powerful message to everyone that what we are is what we do. Day 1 isn't just about talk, it's about action. Yes, Day 1 is risky, it's failure prone and it's unpredictable, but it's something the company passionately believes in.

Questions:

1. What are you doing in terms of culture, talent, metrics and people to ensure you stay Day 1?
2. Ask your team to define what Day 1 looks like to them, and whether they are exceeding or falling behind on their own definition.

Day 2

Recently, I had the opportunity to visit Facebook. Its headquarters are built on the former site of technology giant Sun Microsystems, which was sold to Oracle in 2009 for $7.4 billion. When you arrive, there's a giant poster of the iconic Facebook thumbs up that is actually on the back of the Sun Microsystems logo. Sun was once a $200 billion company with some of the most talented minds in business. I asked myself, what killed its growth and what can your company do to avoid the same fate? The answer is to avoid becoming a Day 2 company. A Day 2 company is the opposite of Day 1. What does a Day 2 company look like? 'Day 2 is stasis. Followed by irrelevance. Followed by excruciating, painful decline.

Followed by death. And that is why Amazon is always Day 1,' says Bezos. A Day 2 company:

- doesn't listen to its customers changing expectations
- is obsessed with doing things right versus doing the right thing
- protects the status quo rather than masters relentless change
- is based on autocratic and rules-based leadership
- drowns in excess bureaucracy
- has a lazy business as its usual mindset.

Day 2 companies are, literally, sleepwalking into oblivion. Theranos, Borders and BlackBerry became Day 2 companies. Who's next?

Questions:

1. Does your organisation turn a blind eye to Day 2? If so, why?
2. Can you think of any other Day 2 companies that were once Day 1?

A TALE OF TWO FUTURES

Are you a Day 1 or Day 2 company? Use the Day 1 practical actions to ensure you stay bold and resilient in the face of accelerating uncertainty.

Day 1 practical actions

1. Encourage failing fast to learn fast.
2. Create employee guidelines that enable speed and autonomy.
3. Fight complexity with simplicity.
4. Build directly responsible individuals (DRIs).
5. Help employees to conduct experiments quickly, cheaply and often.
6. Create multiple paths to yes by using both Type 1 and Type 2 decisions.
7. Prioritise delegation and empowerment at all levels.
8. Focus on data-driven performance but don't forget intuition.
9. Embrace constraints to increase innovation.
10. Use first principles thinking to break problems down and then rebuild them for less.

11. Remember big change starts small.

12. Know the difference between busy work and your best work.

13. Saying 'no' is a productivity tool.

14. Failure and invention are inseparable twins.

15. Stay foolish and hungry when you are successful.

LAUNCH THE BOLD DIMENSION

To launch the bold dimension in your leadership role, do the following.

1.THINK LIKE A STARTUP

Adobe, the software as a service (SaaS) headquartered in California, is a company in which everyone is encouraged to be curious, irrespective of job title. You've probably tried one of Adobe's popular software products, such as Adobe Acrobat Reader or Adobe Photoshop. Founded in 1982, the company has more than 13,500 employees and has continued to reinvent itself to stay at the forefront of technology changes. When Shantanu Narayen became CEO at Adobe in 2007, he saw the warning signals of Day 2, such as inertia, a shift to cloud storage and a saturated user base.

Why don't companies act more like startups? Leaders talk all the time about the need to be more innovative but rarely make it part of their culture. I call it 'innovation theatre'. It's a bit like telling someone to smile and be happy when they're not. And, let's face it, most offices are the worst environments in which to be innovative. When you have to step out of the office to be creative, you know there's a problem. Low ceilings, poor lighting, endless meetings and a lack of fresh air render the brain incapable of a single creative spark. Adobe is different. Shantanu Narayen is a champion of acting boldly. Speaking at a Lean Startup Conference, he tells the story of how Adobe found a new way of innovating. Like most companies, Adobe has transitioned from being a product company to delivering software via cloud technology. In the past, Adobe tested, evaluated and sought feedback from customers on up to a dozen products every year. 'We might spend from $100 up to $1 million on each one of those projects,' says Narayen.

Now the focus is on creating a culture of innovation because nothing is born whole. A new approach, known as Adobe Kickbox, enables them to do several hundred projects for less money than it had cost to do a dozen previously. How has this been possible? Innovation is a long-term investment and Adobe want to build innovators, not just innovations. So the key has been equipping their people with the tools they need to innovate and that means experiencing not only succeeding as an innovator but experiencing failing as an innovator.

Adobe Kickbox is best described as 'innovation in a box'. A red box contains everything an Adobe employee needs to turn an idea into reality, including a $1,000 prepaid credit card, instructions and even a Starbucks coffee gift and confectionary! (Since the fifteenth century, coffee has been touted as the answer for waking up your mind.) The excitement doesn't end with the red box. Once the employee has completed it, he or she is presented with a blue box. What's in it remains a mystery. Adobe Kickbox has 10 principles to think like a startup:

1. Don't follow your passion. Follow your curiosity.
2. Don't wait to be told to do something.
3. Challenge everything.
4. Take risks as a rule, not as the exception.
5. Break the rules, not the law.
6. Cut out the unnecessary.
7. Build a product, not an organisation.
8. Choose courage over comfort.
9. Don't fall in love with ideas. Fall in love with problems.
10. Just get started.

What's for certain is that Adobe not only thinks like a startup but also acts like one and, along the way, it has made its employees fall in love with the company all over again. Today, Adobe is a successful $85 billion SaaS company.

Questions:

1. How could you bring a Silicon Valley startup culture to your organisation?
2. What could you do to speed up learning, experimenting and decision making?

2. APPLY FIRST PRINCIPLES THINKING (FPT)

A hallmark of the bold dimension is a desire to embrace risk. It's about seeing and shaping the future sooner than the competition. Elon Musk is a leader who is ready to dive in, knowing that the obstacles to success will be significant. This means using your brains to imagine a distinct future and then having the belief to back up that vision with laser-like focus and daily effort. Anything worthwhile in business or life will be difficult. These days, leaders expect too many shortcuts and, when they hit a wall, too many of them give up immediately.

Humankind has been launching rockets into space for more than 50 years, often for eye-watering sums of money that only governments can afford. SpaceX founder and CEO Elon Musk has made it possible to build rockets cheaper than it costs to make the movie *Martian* starring Matt Damon. Codenamed BFR (B stands for big, R stands for rocket, I'll leave F to your imagination), Musk has brought the cost of building a rocket down from an industry average of $400 million to less than $90 million. The ultimate goal of putting humanity on Mars by 2030 seems one step closer.

By the age of 46, Elon Musk had innovated and built three revolutionary multibillion dollar companies in completely different fields – PayPal (financial services), Tesla (automotive) and SpaceX (aerospace). At Tesla, Musk holds regular meetings with talk of the new, bold and experimental. During a one-on-one interview with TED Curator Chris Anderson, Musk reveals this missing link which he attributes to Tesla's success. It's called reasoning from 'First Principles'. Musk: 'Well, I do think there's a good framework for thinking. It is physics. You know, the sort of first principles reasoning. Generally, it boils things down to their fundamental truths and reasons up from there, as opposed to reasoning by analogy.'

Through most of our life, we get through life by reasoning by analogy, which essentially means copying what other people do with slight variations. It's simply much easier to think using analogy than first principles. First principles thinking is a physics approach of analysis to problems. The first principles approach – which was first articulated and named by Aristotle – is the practice of identifying the key constraints to achieving a breakthrough in performance and then testing every option possible for eliminating one or more of those constraints.

Musk has applied first principles thinking to Tesla as well. One of the key obstacles to its success was reducing the cost of the battery from the industry standard of $600 per kilowatt hour and getting battery range to exceed 300 miles. Somebody could say, 'Battery packs are really expensive and that's just the way they will always be . . . Historically, it has cost $600 per kilowatt hour. It's not going to be much better than that in the future.' With first principles, you say, 'What are the material constituents of the batteries? What is the stock market value of the material constituents?' It's got cobalt, nickel, aluminium, carbon, some polymers for separation and a seal can.

Break that down on a material basis and say, 'If we bought that on the London Metal Exchange, what would each of those things cost?' It's like $80 per kilowatt hour. So, clearly, you just need to think of clever ways to take those materials and combine them into the shape of a battery cell and you can have batteries that are much, much cheaper than anyone realises.

Questions:

1. How can you use FPT to break out of outdated operating models and assumptions?
2. As a leader and a team, do you make most decisions based on analogy rather than FPT?
3. What assumptions about your business do you need to let go of?

3. FAIL (FROM ACTION I LEARN)

You are bound to fail occasionally, especially when using the bold dimension. In failure are leadership's little secrets: you cannot learn to ride a bike by reading how to ride one. James Dyson produced more than 5,000 failed prototypes before he invented his best-selling Dyson Vacuum Cleaners and Spotify has a 'fail wall' – a platform that publicly celebrates project failures and aims to eliminate fear of failure and learn from mistakes.

Embrace failure as your biggest teacher. It's a vital part of the process of growing as a human being. A real failure is when you make a mistake and don't fix it quickly and start over. The formula for success isn't a mystery. It's a conscious choice to learn from failure. Each wrong choice builds character and strengthens your mindset for the next challenge. Remember, if you're not failing at all, you're probably not trying hard enough.

Questions:

1. Do you reward intelligent failure as one half of success? And is the principle of 'fail fast to learn fast' a core value?
2. Do you unpack the lessons of failure? If not, why not?

4. EMBRACE CONSTRAINTS

Constraints encourage leaders and their teams to think on their feet and rediscover their creativity. Phil Hansen's story is a master class in using the power of constraints. His TED talk, 'Embrace the Shake', has received more than 1.7 million views to date and continues to inspire leaders around the world. Hansen, a pointillist, developed an unruly shake in his hand that kept him from doing what he loved best – drawing art. Devastated, he lost his way, not knowing what the future held. After much soul searching, he decided to see a neurologist, who told him to, 'Embrace the shake and transcend it'.

A mindset that embraces constraints is a concept often mostly overlooked but hugely important for leadership success. Scarcity can lead to resourcefulness and an improved work ethic, pushing everyone to think more creatively about finding the best solution to a problem. Next time you give your team or yourself a challenge, remember Hansen's message that limitations can force us to think bigger. Don't assume that having to make do with less is a hopeless challenge. You can pick up more wonderful lessons from Hansen in his book *Tattoo a Banana: And Other Ways to Turn Anything and Everything into Art*.

Questions:

1. Do you use constraints such as time, scope or money to help teams challenge accepted norms and rethink what is possible?
2. How could you use constraints to push teams to expect more of themselves than they thought was possible?

5. CONNECT THE DOTS

Bold leaders connect the dots for everyone. That means big-picture talk (shaping the future) and detailed talk (making it happen). Paint a vivid picture of the future using storytelling and purpose-oriented words such as 'we', 'our' and 'us' that help the team feel what the late author and physician Oliver Sacks called the 'the three Bs: bonding, belonging and believing'. Strive to help everyone feel part of the purpose and live by it daily. The personal touch matters, so widen the circle of involvement and ask others what the vision personally means to them and how they can support it. A big obstacle today is how to create an environment where everybody brings their best selves to work. The manager era is over. Individuals expect more freedom, autonomy and involvement in all aspects of their roles. If they don't like it, they vote with their feet. That's why a bold purpose has such a transformative effect. Make sure individuals embrace the organisation's purpose and take pride in their personal contributions to it. It's the best way not just to attract talent but to keep it.

Questions:

1. How well do you connect the dots for your team through storytelling and engaging hearts and minds in meaningful ways?
2. Do you communicate more than you engage? Make sure you know the difference. In the age of overload, engaging trumps communication.
3. Do people feel like they have meaning at work?

6. DO FASTER THAN DOUBT

If you want to be *bold*, you must 'do faster than doubt'. Like a boxing match, in the ring on the left corner, we have 'do' – that's the belief that tomorrow can be better than today. In the right corner of the ring, we have the opponent, 'doubt' – that's the fear that you will fail. The faster you act, the more certain you will become, getting quick wins and building up momentum. Wait too long and doubt will grow until it becomes a titanium wall of resistance. You no longer have the mental toughness, the willpower to get up. All this can happen in the blink of an eye. Remember that hope is not a strategy and that you must ring-fence what's essential and then draw the battle lines and get to work.

NEXT IS NOW

What future are you prepared to commit to? It's not easy to close the door and jump into the unknown, bringing your boldest self to your biggest challenges. I've confronted the same challenge when I moved from a rewarding and stable career in consultancy to becoming a writer. Our default setting is to stay in familiar surroundings and accept defeat before even trying. How many times have you thought about a game-changing idea only to let it melt away like snow under the sun? This is known as the 'zone of regret'. Remember, the cost of trying anything in life will never be as painful as never knowing. Facebook Chief Operating Officer Sheryl Sandberg said it best when she delivered a speech to a graduating class of Harvard Business School: 'Get on a rocket ship. When companies are growing quickly and they are having a lot of impact, careers take care of themselves. And when companies aren't growing quickly or their missions don't matter as much, that's when stagnation and politics come in. If you're offered a seat on a rocket ship, don't ask what seat. Just get on.'

The take-home message here? Whatever you're doing, you should be passionate about it. If you're not, then just say no.

As you've now seen, *bold* is the first dimension to thrive as a 3D Leader. It's crucial for leading in a world where to be successful is to evolve. The next superpower is *brave*, which we'll explore in Chapter 3.

KEY MESSAGES

- Embrace disruption as both change and opportunity. Ask yourself: do I have a point of view on the trends and weak signals in my industry and how can I turn risk into opportunity?

- When uncertainty is high, bold questions are the answer. Ask yourself: what are the bravest questions I want to be remembered for?
- Use the power of 10x thinking in every part of your leadership role. Ask yourself: how could I 10x a meeting, a performance review or the way I communicate?
- Apply first principles thinking to challenge outdated assumptions about the world. Ask yourself: which old mindsets and assumptions need to be let go of?
- Not taking a risk is a risk. Ask yourself: do I have a culture of courage or a culture of fear?
- Think like Jeff Bezos. Ask yourself: am I a Day 1 or Day 2 company? Do my financial and non-financial incentives build towards a Day 1 or Day 2 culture?
- The best way to thrive in a future that arrives faster than ever before is by replacing an expert mindset with a beginner's mindset. Ask yourself: when was the last time I learnt something for the first time?

ACTION

If you do only one thing now, think about how you could adopt a beginner's mindset next time you're in a meeting or solving a problem.

The 3D Leader Toolkit for launching the *bold* dimension: use the resources below to move from knowing to doing and accelerate your impact.

Websites

www.thinkwithgoogle.com

www.su.org

www.astroteller.net

www.x.company

www.mindtools.com

Podcasts

Trust Issues by Rachel Botsman

Singularity Hub

Masters of Scale by Reid Hoffman

WorkLife with Adam Grant

Wired Podcasts

TED Talks

Be You. Be True. Be Bold – Professor Daniel Brewster

The Unexpected Benefit of Celebrating Failure – Astro Teller

Designers – think Big! – Tim Brown

Where Good Ideas Come From – Steven Johnson

The Surprising Habits of Original Thinkers – Adam Grant

CHAPTER 3

BRAVE

You can choose comfort or you can choose courage, but you cannot have both.

Brené Brown

In this chapter you will learn to:

- *scale your bravest self*
- *build psychological safety*
- *launch quantum teamwork*
- *reimagine the art of feedback.*

Here's a question. Can you think of a time at work when you had some bad news to share or a concern to raise but held back from speaking because of fear? Fear doesn't make bad news go away, fear makes bad news go into hiding. When I recently asked this question at a conference of over a thousand managers, around 85% put their hands up. Perhaps the other 15% had bad memories. Multiply that by 10,000 or 100,000 people and you can understand why there's a chronic 'speak up' gap in most organisations. It's a powerful question to ask the team you lead, too. I find that if the person asking the question raises their own hand as well, it shows more empathy. The sad truth is holding back and a general reluctance to speak up is the norm in most organisations. Without safety, great ideas are lost, different perspectives are lost, knowledge is lost and great talent is lost. One of the saddest moments for any organisation is wasted talent – the moment when somebody mentally quits the job but continues to work. Now, more than ever, you must create a culture of fearless inquiry and encourage people to overcome the self-imposter syndrome: a common mind-trap in most organisations in which individuals doubt themselves and have a fear of speaking up.

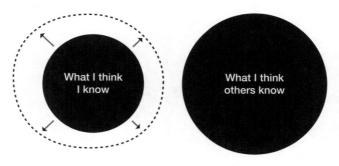

The self-imposter syndrome

Brave is the second dimension of the 3D Leader and is defined as a leader who 'brings their bravest selves to work, speaks up, ask questions, alerts others to concerns and challenges openly'.

Choosing courage over comfort is mission critical for the 3D Leader because there's no crystal ball and it's the best way to reduce the forces of VUCA (volatility, uncertainty, complexity and ambiguity) and help people find pride and meaning in their work. But as any organisation grows, openness and candour are sometimes the first casualties. It becomes easier to leave things unsaid and, typically, there is a failure to act until a situation has reached a crisis point. Silence goes unnoticed, but the costs of fear shouldn't – they are massive. Psychological safety, which is defined as 'a shared belief that a diverse group of people can collaborate and feel comfortable sharing risky new ideas' is vital for building for a high-performing team and is the best way to ensure people are trusted and valued.

Zappos is no stranger to harnessing the brave dimension because it understands that a winning culture means two things:

1. Exceptional customer experiences on the outside.

2. Exceptional employee experience on the inside.

One of its core values is 'to embrace brave'. Headed up by CEO Tony Hsieh, it has won credit around the world for its 3-Day Culture Camps and School of WOW. Employees appreciate that 'to embrace brave' means to be comfortable in your own skin every day and know that the only way to thrive is to be able to speak up about anything on your mind. Does this hold true for you and your organisation?

It's not uncommon for managers to filter bad news to protect the CEO from bad news. The tragedy of two Amnesty International employees committing suicide and the subsequent offering by the board of directors to resign over a toxic work culture is an extreme example of what can go wrong when a culture of silence is the default. Silence is always less risky than voice.

We lack courage rather than answers in most organisations, courage to:

- make a difference
- get behind a great cause
- say no and eliminate the unnecessary
- speak up.

Now is not the time to play it safe. Uncertainty, ambiguity and external forces are creating an operating environment where safety always looks like the right option, although it rarely is. So how do you scale the brave dimension, and how do you build a culture of courage where it's safe to speak up, raise concerns, debate issues and take risks?

CASE STUDY | HiPPOs

Hierarchy and ego are two of the biggest obstacles to psychology safety, as evidenced by the 'HiPPO bias'. 'HiPPO' stands for the 'highest-paid person's opinion' and describes the tendency for employees to always agree with a HiPPO. This can happen at a conference, a meeting, or even the boardroom. In How Google Works, *authors Eric Schmidt and Jonathan Rosenberg write: 'Hippopotamuses are among the deadliest animals, faster than you think and capable of crushing (or biting in half) any enemy in their path. Hippos are dangerous in companies too.' It's human nature to put others on pedestals, especially where power, status, and money are concerned. I once came across a director whose nickname in private circles was 'the shark of sharks'. Needless to say, when he held meetings, there was only one opinion in the room that counted.*

The HiPPO bias can have some nasty side effects; power and status act as self-reinforcing loops: how much status a person has directly affects whether their idea is heard and good ideas get ignored because of someone's job title. Those whose opinions are never challenged run the risk of hubris, and their sense of reality can become distorted. The global financial crisis happened for many reasons; however, there's no question that too many companies decided to follow their HiPPOs rather than make a stand – Royal Bank of Scotland, Arthur Andersen and Lehman Brothers come to mind. The longer we lead, the more difficult it is to remain objective; we get sucked into the day to day, where our default setting can become tunnel vision.

Questions:

1. How would you rate the HiPPO bias at work?
2. What steps can be taken to reduce or eliminate it?
3. How could you make meetings more open and collaborative?

SPEAK UP

Psychological safety is a prerequisite for 3D leadership. There is a growing body of research led by thinkers such as Harvard Professor Amy Edmonson and Wharton School Professor Adam Grant that shows that building psychological safety is critical for helping your team feel alive at work. How alive are you at work?

As conventional hierarchies break down, we are more interdependent on each other now than ever before. Teams who report high levels of psychological safety are at least three times more likely to speak up, share ideas and call out issues. Margaret Heffernan, TED speaker and author of *Beyond Measure*, says: 'In any company, you can have a brilliant bunch of individuals – but what prompts them to share ideas and concerns, contribute to one another's thinking, and warn the group early about potential risks is their connection to one another.' You can't build psychological safety overnight; it's earned on a daily basis. For example, companies such as Danish toy maker Lego build psychological safety through the principle of *hygge* (pronounced 'heu-gah'): teams come together for meals and show up with open minds and a willingness to connect and collaborate.

Psychological safety is not:

- giving unconditional praise
- taking it easy
- a culture of nice, at all expense
- relaxing standards.

Psychological safety is:

- trust between employees
- open-mindedness to change
- curiosity to ask questions and think big
- courage in confronting and overcoming conflict.

Psychological safety is built by leaders who understand that teams can't flourish without mutual respect, safety and trust. To assess whether you have psychological safety in your own team, use the 4C Psychological Safety Tool to identify strengths, manage gaps and flag blind spots.

4C PSYCHOLOGICAL SAFETY TOOL

Nike and Serena Williams recently announced a design challenge for young creatives that will bring new designers to Nike, where they'll work directly with Williams. How is your organisation attracting and amplifying wide, diverse and fresh perspectives? Leaders who embrace diversity of experience, diversity of attitudes and diversity of thinking will have an advantage in adapting to external shocks, which increasingly threaten the survival of their organisations. The 4C psychological safety tool looks at four essential builders of high psychological safety: curiosity safety, challenger safety, collaboration safety and culture safety.

1. **Curiosity safety:** how safe is it to follow your curiosity at work? To learn, experiment and fail in your organisation? When you're exploring ideas to improve the business or the customer experience, fear is at its highest and can sabotage your best efforts to try something new. Stop worrying about the rate of failure because, as long as those failures are cheap, you can afford a lot of them. As the saying goes, 'fail fast, fail cheap and move on'. Curiosity safety means it's safe to adopt an experimental attitude, test out the riskiest assumptions and use failure as a tool to learn from your own and others' mistakes. Without curiosity safety, the gap between what you know and what you want to know is likely to freeze.

2. **Challenger safety:** how safe is it to have tough conversations and challenge others about issues that matter? Perceptions of power, status and trust affect how much teams speak, listen and respect each other. To defeat groupthink, individuals must be rewarded for straight talking at all levels. Challenger safety means it's safe for individuals to speak up about their concerns, disagree openly and challenge each other, no matter what the person's hierarchical status is. The opportunity to have a voice and be heard, even when there is a dissenting viewpoint, is mandatory for challenger safety. Everyone in your organisation should feel safe to take a stand on something that is important and be able to raise it well without fear of criticism or judgement.

3. **Collaboration safety:** how safe is it to openly share information and work with others across the whole organisation? Collaboration safety is confident vulnerability – the glue that holds people together from chance encounters to more formal work relationships. It's the foundation of every human action, relationship and interaction and helps us to get the best from each other. The foundation of collaboration safety is trust, which lies not in grand gestures but in everyday actions, words and interactions: speaking openly and honestly versus tiptoeing around half-truth or doing what is right versus what is easy, in order to avoid discomfort. We all have the power to act in more trustworthy ways. Without mutual trust, it's more difficult to collaborate and more difficult to get things done.

4. **Culture safety:** if I asked you what's the one thing you could do differently tomorrow to make your organisation a better place to work, where would you start? The answer is probably culture. Corporate culture can seem like a fuzzy word but I define it as the values, beliefs and behaviours practised in your organisation, especially when you're

not in the room. Culture is like pouring concrete. It can take a while to set but then is much more difficult to change afterwards. I took the pulse of over 1,200 business leaders globally. An overwhelming 84% agreed that culture is critical for business success and 60% agreed it was more important than strategy or the business model. The bad news was that more than half the group reported that culture was not effectively managed and was not even on the leadership agenda. The bottom line is that culture is seen as incredibly important but mismanaged and undervalued in most organisations.

1. Curiosity safety	3. Collaboration safety

1. We learn from mistakes
  1 2 3 4 5
	1. We call out team issues
	  1 2 3 4 5

2. We test out new ideas
  1 2 3 4 5
	2. We can ask for help from anyone
	  1 2 3 4 5

3. It's safe to say I don't know
  1 2 3 4 5
	3. We share information openly
	  1 2 3 4 5

2. Challenger safety	4. Culture safety

1. We deliver difficult messages
  1 2 3 4 5
	1. Our core values are lived
	  1 2 3 4 5

2. We speak up about concerns
  1 2 3 4 5
	2. Our culture rewards radical candour
	  1 2 3 4 5

3. We disagree with others
  1 2 3 4 5
	3. We understand what makes our culture unique
	  1 2 3 4 5

Questions:

1. Do you have high levels of psychological safety in your team? If not, why not?

2. What are the current levels of curiosity safety, challenger safety, collaboration safety and culture safety?

3. What are the reasons for the psychological safety strengths and gaps?

4. How can you role model psychological safety? For example go first, be open and show vulnerability.

5. How do you reward those who show courage to speak up, share ideas and challenge others?

CASE STUDY

Psychological safety cuts to the heart of Formula One (F1). This hyper competitive sport is all about winning and is a great example to other sports (and industries) that aspire to reach the top of their game. Every week, the drivers test the limits of human and super-car performance around the track using a constant cycle: design, refine, race and repeat. The pressure is intense and unrelenting. Here are some of the most jaw-dropping facts:

- *More than 1,000 data points in the car are analysed during a race, helping to improve every time-sensitive aspect of the car.*
- *30k design changes in a season.*
- *7.5k unique parts.*
- *1 million parts manufactured.*
- *A gear change is 50x faster than the blink of an eye.*

Few teams have dominated F1 like the Mercedes AMG Petronas Formula One Team headed up by the Austrian, Torger Christian 'Toto' Wolff. In the last five years alone, they have built some of the fastest cars in Grand Prix history and hold the record for winning 20 poles (the highest percentage ever in a single season of F1 at 95.2%) and F1 Champion Lewis Hamilton has won the World Championship six times so far and is well on his way to eclipsing Michael Schumacher's F1 record.

At Mercedes, psychological safety is the difference that makes the difference. The headquarters, nestled in the English countryside, is a showcase for excellence. There's a high-performing building designed by world-renowned architects. Most office buildings undermine innovation: low ceilings, poor artificial light and physical silos on different floors render most teams fragmented and lacking the type of unity required to win. Mercedes stands out in a world where most companies are trapped in traditional twentieth-century mindsets. Its headquarters has plenty of open spaces for chance encounters to occur and outside there's woodland for informative 'walk and talk' meetings and even a lake to help busy minds unplug. The whole building is designed to encourage psychological safety and help a diverse group of people feel safe to share risky new ideas about what needs to change in order to keep winning.

Building psychological safety in teams sounds like an abstract idea, but it derives from some deliberate actions:

- *Be more available to your employees.*
- *Share your mistakes and what you learned from them.*
- *Encourage team members to ask for help and guidance.*
- *Reward teams that report errors rather than those who ignore them.*

Take time to measure how many of the above steps you follow and know that investment in time and effort will be worthwhile.

QUANTUM TEAMWORK

Most teams are not teams. They are just groups of individuals without a single collective purpose. The new science of teamwork requires a team mindset known as quantum teamwork. As the name implies, quantum teamwork is defined as 'a quantum-leap improvement in performance while transforming the mindsets of employees and thus the culture of the organisation':

- High diversity and high psychological safety.
- We beats me.
- Co-creation beats control.
- Teams beat groups.
- Culture beats strategy.
- Engagement beats communication.
- Shared values beat no values.

Quantum teamwork arises when groups work together to be smarter and perform better; it's the team capacity for high performance. Thomas W. Malone is a professor of management at the MIT Sloan School of Management and a founding director of the MIT Center for Collective Intelligence. The Center's mission is to unlock the science behind the deep phenomenon of humans working together or humans and computers working together in ways that will help us understand how to create new kinds of human or human and computer cooperatives or collective intelligences.

Faculty members are drawn from many different parts of MIT, including the Media Lab, the Department of Brain and Cognitive Sciences and the Computer Science and Artificial Intelligence Lab. Their aim is to identify what makes some teams faster, smarter and better than others. What does it take to tap the collective intelligence of your own team, and how can leaders do that? Malone and a team of MIT researchers studied a raft of factors, such as psychological safety, personality types, teamwork and gender that turn a group into a smart, high-performing team. In two studies, published in the journal *Science*, researchers grouped 697 volunteers into teams of two to five members. Each team was required to work together to complete a range of cognitive tasks, from brainstorming to teamwork and problem solving. What they found was that individual intelligence (as measured by IQ) was not as important as they had assumed. Nor did teams with more extroverted people or individual stars make a noticeable difference to the group's overall success. What did matter was empathy, the ability to read others' emotions, trust and frequent communication with equal respect for each team member's opinion.

Quantum teams were distinguished by three characteristics: first, their members contributed more equally to the team's discussion, rather than letting one or two people dominate the group. Second, their members scored higher on a test called Reading the Mind in the Eyes, which measures how well people can read complex emotional states from images of faces with only the eyes visible. Finally, teams with high diversity and high psychological safety outperformed teams with low diversity and low psychological safety.

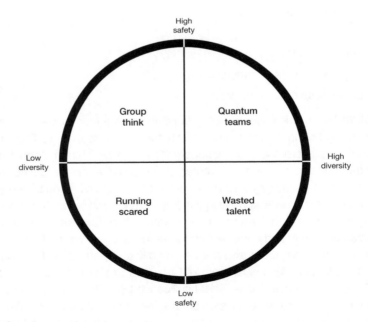

Quantum teams

To increase quantum teamwork in your own organisation, do this:

1. **Crowdsource ideas.** Harness the wisdom of the team at all levels of your organisation and build a culture of learning where it's safe to test, explore and experiment. For example, at Amazon, Jeff Bezos asks three questions: How original is the idea and what problem is it solving? How scaleable is the idea because it's important to think big? And what is the project return on investment of this idea? Innovations such as Amazon Prime and 1-Click purchasing are a direct result of building a culture where employees understand that they now compete on imagination. What platforms do you have in place to crowdsource ideas from both employees and customers?

2. **Idea recognition.** Great ideas can come from anywhere in your organisation. The problem is most organisations are made up of Chief Idea Killers, Directors of Bureaucracy and Vice-Presidents of 'No'. Build interactive channels that make it easy for ideas to be validated quickly and where good mistakes are never wasted. At the music platform SoundCloud, there are monthly Hackathons for people to find solutions to pain points that cause friction for customers on the outside and employees on the inside. What steps could you take to recognise and reward employees to think and act like innovators?

3. **Build social capital.** Most leaders communicate but don't engage. Using different channels builds up the all-important social capital, which binds a team together emotionally and psychologically. This strengthens mutual trust and sharpens emotion-reading skills for the whole team. Imagine social capital as a bank where you make regular credits and debits. Without it, you don't get the tough debates that problems demand and the fresh ideas and new perspectives that will propel a company forward. Not speaking up speaks volumes. I have adopted the Japanese principle of *ba* – to get involved and transcend one's own limited perspective or boundary. Put another way, *ba* refers to a physical, virtual or mental space shared by two or more individuals. You can unlock the collective intelligence embedded in *ba* by providing diverse meeting spaces and the creative freedom to unshackle from boring routines. Do you have physical spaces that enable the Japanese principle of *ba* to occur?

4. **Increase high diversity and high psychological safety.** The opportunity to have a voice and be heard, even when there is a dissenting view, is unlocking the power of quantum teams. Job titles, hierarchy and self-imposter syndrome are just some of the barriers

that erode success and can be overcome only with high diversity and high psychological safety. In a recent talk at New York University, I emphasised the power of diverse teams *and* psychological safety. Successful leaders pull together people with different perspectives and ways of seeing the world. What tools can you use to scale both high diversity and high psychological safety?

CASE STUDY

Jack Dorsey is known at Twitter for being the last to speak at meetings. He prefers to listen to what others have to say without biasing them by giving his opinion first. He says, 'inside a large company you need multiple paths to yes'. Dorsey delegates and empowers others to experiment and take risks through a technique called 'future back' to tap the collective intelligence of the company. Rather than starting with an idea for a product, you start with an idea for a customer and imagine that product has already been launched. Any employee with a big idea is encouraged to design a press release that includes a customer-impact statement, key questions and perspectives from different business areas. The press release is a good way to help employees to explain to the organisation what their ideas are about, and how their solutions are going to solve a customer problem. The press release itself is a gut-check for whether or not the product is worth building. If the team is not excited about reading it, then the document needs to be revised or perhaps the idea should be revisited altogether. As the team begins development, the press release serves as a guide for the team to reflect on and compare with what is being built.

Here's an example outline for the press release:

- *Heading: name the product in a way the reader (i.e. your target customers) will understand.*
- *Sub-heading: describe who the market for the product is and what benefit they get. One sentence only underneath the title.*
- *Summary: give a summary of the product and the benefit. Assume the reader will not read anything else, so make this paragraph good.*
- *Problem: describe the problem your product solves.*
- *Solution: describe how your product elegantly solves the problem.*
- *Quote from you: a quote from a spokesperson in your company.*
- *How to get started: describe how easy it is to get started.*

- *Customer quote: provide a quote from a hypothetical customer that describes how they experienced the benefit.*

- *Closing and call to action: wrap it up and give pointers where the reader should go next.*

Iterating on a press release is a lot quicker and less expensive than iterating on the product itself.

Questions:

1. How could you apply the Future Back tool in your organisation?
2. Do you always speak first in meetings or empower others to go first?
3. Are there multiple paths to yes? How easy is it for new ideas to come from anywhere in the business?

FEEDBACK REIMAGINED

Leaders give feedback, feedback drives behaviour and behaviour produces results. But are you unlocking the huge benefits of feedback? It's impossible to thrive unless you can deliver relevant, timely feedback. Feedback about performance, feedback about job purpose, feedback about direction and feedback about motivation or behaviours.

EVERYDAY PERFORMANCE AND DEVELOPMENT FEEDBACK AT A GLANCE

1. Constructive feedback on performance, standards or behaviours.
2. Progress against objectives.
3. Difficult situations, e.g. conflict.
4. Well-being and ways of working.
5. Career development.

Feedback is an important tool for shaping behaviours and fostering learning but it's also a sign of high psychological safety. When it feels safe to ask for and give feedback, people report higher levels of well-being and trust. Feedback shows you care about learning and growth. It's a trust multiplier and, yet, in most organisations, there is a feedback famine. And is your organisations exceeding, meeting or falling behind on expectations of feedback? My research of 1,000 leaders showed that only 37% report that feedback is delivered consistently and 63% agreed with the statement 'we're falling behind on how we deliver feedback'.

CASE STUDY

What do the best leaders do differently? That's a question Google spent considerable time trying to answer. Using data analytics, the company discovered 13 leadership behaviours that the best leaders demonstrated. How would you rank? And how would your employees rate you? The questions below show which behaviours and traits Google feels great leaders possess in order of importance.

Consider how your employees would rate you: using a 1 (strongly agree) to 5 (strongly disagree) scale.

1. *My leader gives me actionable feedback that helps me improve my performance.*
2. *My leader does not 'micromanage' (get involved in details that should be handled at other levels).*
3. *My leader shows consideration for me as a person.*
4. *The actions of my leader show that he/she values the perspective I bring to the team, even if it is different from his/her own.*
5. *My leader keeps the team focused on our priority results/deliverables.*
6. *My leader regularly shares relevant information from his/her manager and senior leaders.*
7. *My leader has had a meaningful discussion with me about career development in the past six months.*
8. *My leader communicates clear goals for our team.*
9. *My leader has the technical expertise (e.g. coding in tech, selling in global business, accounting in finance) required to effectively manage me.*
10. *I would recommend my leader to peers.*
11. *I am satisfied with my leader's overall performance as a manager.*
12. *What would you recommend your leader keep doing?*
13. *What would you have your leader change?*

Every question focuses on soft skills, except question No. 9, which asks employees to rate their manager's hard skills. The evaluation predominately measures not what leaders know but how they do their jobs using soft skills: emotional intelligence, coaching, feedback, communication and empathy. The number one takeaway is that the best leaders understand that actionable feedback is a gift.

Questions:

1. Answer the Google leader's questionnaire. How will you strengthen your top three leadership behaviours?

2. Ask your direct team to score you using the Google Leader's Questionnaire. What blind spots were highlighted and what steps will you take to address them?

3. Ask your manager to score you as well. Which leadership behaviours require the most attention today?

WHY FEEDBACK MATTERS

1. Gives me purpose and direction: 49%.
2. Helps me perform better: 73%.
3. Makes me feel valued: 93%.

The human and organisational implications of this are significant. Poorly delivered feedback or simply a lack of feedback erodes trust, respect and psychological safety, which are the building blocks of a high-performing team.

How do you deliver feedback effectively on the issues that really matter? From what you say to how you say it, to dealing with tricky conversations and difficult messages, it's clear that the gap is too high for feedback.

THE SEVEN DEADLY SINS OF FEEDBACK

How many of the feedback sins have you committed in your career? The best way to avoid feedback sins is through self-awareness, empathy and listening. The seven deadly sins of feedback are:

1. No feedback.
2. Too general.
3. Too personal.
4. Too long.

5. Too directive.

6. No empathy.

7. No follow-up.

A PRACTICAL GUIDE TO FEEDBACK

Feedback is a skillset and a mindset. You can use the AID practical feedback tool below to deliver timely, relevant and outcome-led feedback that shows you care personally about individuals' learning, growth and well-being.

A Align on outcomes
Align: care personally and agree on outcomes
Examples:

- I'd like to help you develop XYZ.
- I'd like to have a conversation with you about XYZ.
- Let's catch up about X.
- I think there's an opportunity to grow/develop A.

I Improve performance
Improve: move towards solutions
Examples:

- What could you do differently?
- How can I help you make a bigger impact?
- How about trying XYZ?
- What options do you have?
- What could you change?
- What else could you do?

D Decide
Decide: gain commitment to next steps
Examples:

- What will you do to move forward?
- What are the next steps?
- Who can support you?
- Is there anything else you need?
- What does success look like?

CASE STUDY

Ed Catmull's big idea, the Pixar Brain Trust, helps build a feedback culture. Catmull is the former CEO of Pixar, the animation giant responsible for ground-breaking films such as The Incredibles, Monsters Inc., *and* Toy Story. *Leaders adopt daily reviews or 'dailies', a process for giving and getting immediate feedback in a positive way. Its purpose is to put hierarchy to the side and focus on straight talk about the learning, growth and performance. Individuals want to know how they're doing. One of the most useful actions you can take today is to give your team regular progress updates. Frequency really does matter. A once-a-year review in an age where most look at their mobile phone more than 50 times a day no longer works. Make sure you declare what really matters, and why, and then ensure you deliver on those expectations.*

FEEDBACK SCENARIOS

Use the five feedback scenarios below with your team to increase your confidence at everyday feedback. It can be a very powerful learning experience to conduct two 90-second 'acts'. It relaxes the group and they learn that it's all too easy to commit the seven deadly sins without realising it, so they learn not to do them in real life.

Feedback scenarios example

- Act 1: demonstrate how *not* to give feedback using examples from the seven deadly sins.

- Act 2: demonstrate best practice using the AID tool.

    Scenario 1: one of your new team members spoke too fast in a presentation. You want to help her improve. *What happens next?*

    Scenario 2: one of your co-workers has written a sloppy email to a new client into which you were cc'd. The spelling and punctuation need improving. *What happens next?*

    Scenario 3: one of your team is always arriving late to work. Some colleagues have expressed a concern about the person's well-being. *What happens next?*

Scenario 4: one of your team has not been contributing at meetings. Some colleagues have commented he has lost his motivation. You wish to resolve the situation. *What happens next?*

Scenario 5: your boss hasn't given you any feedback on your performance for more than six months. You'd like to ask for some specific feedback on how you're doing and what could be better. *What happens next?*

Checklist

1. **Respect:** avoid the seven deadly sins of feedback by using the AID tool.
2. **Listen:** ask open questions, signal empathy and help individuals to find their own solution.
3. **Focus:** look for coachable moments in your team, flag blind spots and leverage strengths.
4. **Grow:** use everyday feedback to accelerate learning, growth and performance.
5. **Challenge:** use everyday feedback to get the best out of each other and avoid a culture of silence.

CASE STUDY

Courage helps people to 'tell it how it is' without fear of recrimination. Yannick Theler is a leader on a mission to scale courage in everything he does, from giving feedback and running great meetings to building a winning culture. He is the Founder and Managing Director of Ubisoft Abu Dhabi, a part of Ubisoft, the leading games developer responsible for ground-breaking games such as Assassin's Creed, CSI: Hidden Crimes, and Far Cry. Remember, 'your culture is always on, 24/7 – and it's either growing or dying', says Theler. 'We hire for skill, talent and culture contribution, and we encourage feedback every day by making it safe to speak up, ask questions, challenge one another, and share ideas. The studio has over 27 nationalities working together in teams, which creates incredible ideas and energy. The magic happens when different mindsets and cultures collide.'

Below he outlines eight principles for scaling courage:

1. *Courage equals risk, resilience and psychological safety.*
2. *Everyone must have the freedom to communicate with anyone.*
3. *It must be safe for everyone to offer ideas.*
4. *We build an 'everyone culture' through speaking up, asking questions and giving feedback.*
5. *Model and reward candid feedback by using expressions such as 'I want to hear from you' and 'What support do you need from me?'.*
6. *Share humility and vulnerability with others and respond positively when people show the courage to speak up.*
7. *Don't hire for culture fit. This can increase groupthink. Rather, hire for culture contribution to increase diversity of ideas.*
8. *Values equal results. We get the best out of our team and one another by holding everyone to the highest standards and by attracting and growing our talent using ELITE values: edge, learning, imagination, team and energy. It's important that everyone can express themselves through these values and have the psychological safety to tell it how it is. A speak-up culture beats a culture of silence every time.*

Theler uses ask-me-anything (AMA) meetings to put hierarchy to the side and focus on straight talk about the ideas and direction of a game. It's not a brainstorming meeting per se. Rather, its role is to be completely open, honest and direct about content and ideas. 'Let's face it,' says Theler. 'Most meetings in most companies fall behind on expectations. At the studio, we use a "meeting wheel" inspired by Amazon Web Services (AWS) that gives everyone a chance to have a voice and boosts ROI – not return on investment but return on ideas, which is the DNA of everything we do here.'

Everyone offers support but, crucially, no one has the authority to tell each other's team what to do. At the end of a meeting, they must decide what to use and what to ignore. Says Theler: 'When one of the team is in need of assistance, they convene the group (and anyone else they think would be valuable) and show the current version of the game in progress. This is followed by a lively give-and-take discussion, which is all about making the game better. There's no ego. Nobody pulls any punches to be polite. This works because all the attendees have come to trust and respect one another. They know it's far better to learn about problems from colleagues when there's still time to fix them than from the audience after it's too late. The problem-solving powers of this group are immense and inspirational to watch.'

An Ask Me Anything meeting is different from a standard meeting. It brings together a group of leaders who are explicitly asked to be candid, to speak the truth on a daily basis. The net effect is individuals taking more pride in their work and more responsibility for their decisions. For Theler, everybody is searching for their who, what, and why. 'Visualise this thing that you want,' he said. 'See it, feel it and believe in it. Make your mental blueprint, and then begin to build.' Now that's a winning culture.

Questions:

1. How could you incorporate an Ask Me Anything meeting?
2. How would your team describe your culture in three words? Does it match your definition?
3. Do you hire and reward for culture contribution? If not, why not?

EMPATHY

I believe an important part of the *brave* dimension is the art of human connection. How well do you connect with your team personally? When I asked 1,000 leaders this question, only 44% agreed their manager knew them well and 63% cited a lack of emotional intelligence as the reason they did not connect well. Jack Ma of Alibaba says that, in the past, work was about muscles, now it's about brains and, in the future, it will be about the heart. Empathy is the language of leadership and is a proven way to build high psychological safety, no matter what the situation or challenge. Empathy increases understanding, collaboration and conflict resolution. Top empathetic companies generate more earnings than the rest. Their secret: they treat people as human beings, not human resources.

The problem is in a world where battles for our attention are at record levels and, when 1/5 leaders report burnout, it's all too easy for empathy to take a back seat. The elevator test is a simple and fun way to test your current levels of empathy. Next time you walk into an elevator, check to see whether you: 1. Keep the doors open for somebody else who is approaching; or 2. Press the button frantically to close the door in the face of the person just before they get there.

My research of 1,000 leaders showed that 90% agree empathy is important – one of the best ways to thrive – and, yet, only 33% said it was a current strength. For me, empathy is about 'we, not me'. Empathy begins with attention, which is one of the rarest and purest forms of generosity a leader can give today in our 'always on' workplaces. It's about putting yourself in the shoes of those around you and seeing the world from their perspective. I recently saw Richard Branson do exactly this at a conference when he took his shoes off and said it's impossible to understand your team and your customers without walking in their shoes. When's the last time you walked in somebody else's shoes?

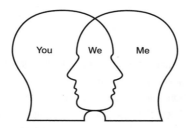

Decoding empathy

EMPATHY BUILDERS

- Listening
- Attention
- Interest
- Perspective taking
- Appreciation
- Patience
- Compassion.

Leaders scale empathy in different ways. At Starbucks, when making decisions about the future, CEO Kevin Johnson uses the empty chair technique when making high stakes decisions about the future direction of the business. The empty chair represents the customer. Howard Schultz, the former Chairman and CEO of Starbucks, always ensured there were two empty chairs at every board meeting. The first chair represents the customers, their thoughts, needs and feelings. The second chair is a bit more surprising. This chair is for Starbucks employees. Schultz deeply understood that employees are partners in the success of the company and, without factoring them into the equation, the company has no chance of succeeding. Whether empty chairs are a nice idea or a useful practice, focusing on employees' needs is one of the more crucial keys to success.

At JPMorgan Chase, CEO Jamie Dimon believes that empathy can't be created artificially and begins with relationships. One in seven banking customers around the world has a visual or hearing disability, which affects their ability to shop online. The leaders at JPMorgan wanted their teams to step into the shoes of the 1/7 clients who are visually or hearing impaired. Using VR equipment dubbed the 'empathy enhancer', individuals can step into the shoes of their clients and see the world from their perspective.

CASE STUDY

Adam Galinsky is a Social Psychologist at Columbia Business School, known for his research on leadership, power, negotiations, decision-making, diversity and ethics. The question Galinsky wanted to answer was: Does power decrease empathy in leaders? To set the experiment up, he has devised a simple test which he believes can measure a person's ability to take another's perspective in a complex social situation. The experiment involves participants tracing the capital letter 'E' on their forehead. Step 1. Hold up the index finger of your dominant hand and draw a capital E on your forehead. Do this as quickly as possible, without stopping to think. Step 2. Now, consider the E you drew. If you'd had a marker and had actually drawn the letter on your forehead, would someone looking at your face see a regular E or a backward one. Those who write a self-E, so it makes sense to themselves, are said to have less empathy and tend toward their own perspective – a trait common in powerful figures. Those who write an E-to-others, if the letter is written so it makes sense to others but not yourself, are shown to have more empathy and take the perspective of others into consideration when making decisions. Galinksy discovered that leaders who felt powerful were about three times as likely to draw the backward E compared to those who'd been made to feel less powerful. And this suggests, Galinsky argues, that power makes people more focused on their own unique vantage point and oblivious to the perspective of others. The biggest mistake leaders can make is believing that considering others' perspectives is a sign of weakness. Rather, the opposite is true – it's a sign of strength that leaders can exert influence and also show empathy for other people's feelings.

Questions:

1. How would your team rate existing levels of empathy in yourself and your fellow leaders? Would customers describe your company as empathetic?
2. When was the last time you showed empathy in your leadership role?
3. What steps are you taking to build empathy as a mindset and skillset in your team?
4. Is empathy built into your customer's journey from zero friction experiences to personalisation?

THE SISU LAB

How do you transform barriers to frontiers? The 3D Leader has what the Finnish call *sisu*, a flair for 'extraordinary determination and resoluteness in the face of extreme adversity'. It takes *sisu* to stand at the door when a big angry bear is on the other side. That bear could be your competition or even a deep-seated inner fear holding you back from a better future. Emilia Lahti heads up The Sisu Lab and is a distinguished researcher of the Finnish construct of *sisu*. She holds an Applied Positive Psychology Masters Degree from the University of Pennsylvania and has been mentored in the fields of grit, self-control and positive psychology by world-renowned thought leaders Dr Martin Seligman and Dr Angela Duckworth.

Lahti is the embodiment of *sisu*. Her work stems from a traumatic experience that made her rethink her whole life and, ultimately, find her true calling: helping others. In the long term, she wants to identify practical ways for the cultivation of *sisu* within various contexts, from being a leader to recovering from traumatic experiences. She writes: 'Evolution comes before survival only in the dictionary. We are creatures of reason, programmed to preserve energy and maintain equilibrium. However, in order to not merely survive but to thrive, we must occasionally crank our comfort-o-meter to the red zone. Having an "action mindset" will help you bear the initial discomfort and reap the ultimate rewards.'

You can unlock your inner *sisu* by doing more of the following:

- Leaders are only as strong as the adversity they overcome.
- Make a choice to take action. Decide comes from the Latin word *decidere* which means 'to let go'.
- Remember FAIL stands for from action I learn. Failure is always learning in disguise.

- Stay in the present moment – don't create extra problems that don't yet exist or get trapped in the past by over-analysing what can't be changed.
- Explore the edges of your comfort zone. Sometimes, the obstacle becomes the path and within every obstacle is an opportunity to learn and grow.

CASE STUDY

Harry Potter *author J.K. Rowling is a prominent example of* sisu. *She was rejected more than 130 times before she got noticed. According to legend, one publisher even told her 'not to give up the day job'. We know what happened after that. The* Harry Potter *series became one of the most successful film franchises ever, grossing more than $6 billion.*

On receiving an honorary degree from Harvard University, Rowling gave a heartfelt commencement speech titled 'The Fringe Benefits of Failure, and the Importance of Imagination'. She told the audience: 'Ultimately, we all have to decide for ourselves what constitutes failure. But the world is quite eager to give you a set of criteria, if you let it. Failure means a stripping away of the inessential. I stopped pretending to myself to be anything other than what I was, and began to direct all my energy into finishing the only work that mattered to me. Had I really succeeded at anything else, I might never have found the determination to succeed in the one arena where I believe I truly belonged. Rock bottom became the solid foundation on which I built my life.' Rowling is now a successful role model for millions of people around the world.

Questions:

1. How can you manage adversity in your own leadership role?
2. What steps can you take to unlock your inner *sisu*?
3. Think of a setback or challenge you have faced. How did it help you grow as a leader?

To scale the brave dimension and bring your best and bravest self to work, follow these actions:

1. Reimagine feedback

Today's best performance is tomorrow's baseline. Be ready to innovate all your internal processes including your annual performance review. Many forward-thinking companies, such as Accenture, Deloitte and HubSpot have already eschewed this much over-hyped process in favour of more frequent real-time feedback based on individual assignments. Allocating so much effort and resources on a once-a-year process runs the risk of it simply becoming a bureaucratic tick-box exercise or worse, delaying vital performance-related conversations that should happen daily. As a leader, you have to mesh an individual's sense of purpose with that of the organisation. Doug Conant, former CEO of Campbell Soup, in a *Harvard Business Review* article, writes: 'Your employees are not mind-readers.' Make sure you declare what really matters and why and then ensure you deliver on those expectations. At Pixar, the animation company, leaders adopt daily reviews or 'dailies', a process for giving and getting immediate feedback in a positive way. Individuals want to know how they're doing. One of the most useful actions you can take today is to give your team regular progress updates. Frequency really does matter. A once-a-year review in an age where most look at their mobile phone more than 50 times per day no longer works.

Questions:

1. Is your current feedback process meeting or exceeding expectations?
2. Is feedback a strength? If not, what's the one thing you can do differently to improve daily feedback?
3. What are the biggest sins of feedback in your organisation? And what measures can you take to remove them?

2. Stop bad meetings

Most leaders are really bad at running meetings. In my own experience of attending hundreds of meetings, I quickly evolved from FOMO (fear of missing out) to JOMO (joy of missing out). I observed that a lot were good at top-down style communication, the kind the military invented, but very rarely were good at extracting questions, concerns and ideas from employees who knew the company and its customers best. Many leaders are still trapped in bad meetings syndrome which means 'having meetings about meetings'. Opportunities are missed, conversations are wasted, and teams become invisible. The 3D Leader is different. It places a huge amount of value on talent and ideas, always looking for better ways to extract the best thinking and creativity from others.

Intermittent meetings work well for meetings of up to 10 people and increase personal contributions by giving everyone equal participation and a voice to fully express oneself. One of the most frustrating parts of anyone's career is trying to cut through all the barriers to communicate ideas and problems to the actual decision maker. For many people, there are an unconscionable number of obstacles to overcome in order to have a voice and be heard. Silence is always the safer option. With intermittent meetings, there are three simple steps to follow:

1. Frame a question or problem to the group first.

2. Allocate five minutes of 'deep thinking' time to allow the participants to write down their own point of view. This step is important to give everybody the time and respect to think.

3. Invite a participant to share their ideas and then ask them to nominate somebody else. This boosts trust, psychological safety and reduces groupthink and self-similarity bias where we, unwittingly, speak more to those who are more similar to us.

Questions:

1. How many meetings do you go to every week? Is it too many?

2. How could you make meetings shorter and more energising?

3. Which meetings could you eliminate today?

---

3. Diversify everything

Diversity is not only an ethical priority – it can also make teams more resilient in the face of adversity. When diversity is high, leaders report higher levels of innovation and engagement because they increase the capacity for original ideas by expanding the range of viewpoints and options available. We have a long way to go, though. Even as diversity initiatives and the #MeToo movement work to balance power dynamics across a range of industries and workplaces, the statistics on women in leadership roles tell a woeful story. In the UK, there are just 6 women CEOs – and 16 CEOs called John – in the FTSE 100 and only 25 out of 500 women CEOs in the USA.

Did you know, a new Forbes study reports that the top five women leaders in the world today are:

1. CEO Marillyn Hewson at Lockheed Martin.
2. CEO Mary Barra of at General Motors.
3. CEO Abigail Johnson at Fidelity Investments.
4. CEO Ginni Rometty at IBM.
5. CEO Gail Boudreaux at Anthem Inc.

The situation is not good for startups, either. According to data from PitchBook, female founders received 2.2% of $130 billion in VC funding. A McKinsey Global Institute report finds that $12 trillion could be added to global GDP by 2025 by advancing women's equality. As the speed of change accelerates, it's becoming increasingly clear that having diverse and inclusive teams isn't just a moral imperative, it's increasingly necessary to stay on top and you can't do that if half the planet are ignored.

My research on diverse and inclusive decision making to understand just how much improvement is possible shows that inclusive teams report making better decisions up to 87% of the time and decisions made and executed by diverse teams delivering 60% better results. Diversity is not a nice to have. It's a must have.

Questions:

1. Do you think about diversity from the start?
2. Do you hire for both diversity and inclusion?
3. Do you celebrate employee differences?
4. What's the boldest action you've taken to reduce gender bias?

4. Scale trust

Without trust, there's no collaboration and without collaboration there's no value. I spend a lot of time helping leaders build, manage or recover trust. In the last year, 10 out of 15 industries have reported a material decline in trust with their customers due to data breaches and cyber crime. The writer George Orwell would have relished these times. Fake news, false facts, alternative facts, meme warfare and internet trolls, to name just a few.

Trust builders:	Trust destroyers:
■ expertise	■ ego
■ integrity	■ complacency
■ reliability	■ inaction
■ empathy	■ inconsistency
■ respect.	■ dishonesty.

Leaders can earn peoples' trust by prioritising it alongside growth and profitability and leading by the credo that trust is won and lost on a daily basis by matching what you say with what you do and engaging everybody in the direction of the business. Relationships equal results. As a leader, you must be ready to leverage each trust builder with all your stakeholders by following three steps:

Step 1. Measure the current levels of trust with your employees and customers and know where you stand as a leader.

Step 2. Bake trust into the culture by leading with context more than control.

Step 3. Elevate the importance of trust across the whole stakeholder mix from employees to suppliers and customers.

Questions:

1. Have you identified the existing levels of trust in your team?
2. Which of the trust destroyers have you identified at your organisation? What preventive action will you take?
3. What's the one thing you can start doing today as a leader to scale trust in your team?
4. Are my intentions aligned with yours?
5. Do my actions match my words?

5. Hire originals

The French have an expression called '*déformation professionnelle*', which means the way your profession can subtly warp your judgement so that you can see things from only one perspective. *Don't hire for culture fit. Hire for culture contribution.* Seek out people who look at the world differently, see around corners or bring surprising new perspectives.

Some of the biggest companies are making autism a hiring priority and organisations such as JPMorgan Chase and McKinsey are stepping up efforts to grow these untapped talent pools. Have the courage to put hiring originals centre stage in your organisation because it's when different mindsets collide that new connections and breakthroughs are made. Hiring for diversity and building a team of originals is one of the fastest routes to faster innovation and a heathier human-first culture.

Questions:

1. Do you hire for culture fit or culture contribution?
2. What's the biggest action you've taken to widen the talent pool in your organisation?
3. What talent strategies do you have to grow and retain your top performers?
4. How would you rate the quality of your onboarding? Can it be improved?

6. Build a strong mind

Leadership is a decision. The brave dimension is a decision: you choose to learn from the challenges or let them defeat you. To achieve greatness, you have to fail greatly. Hollywood producer and director Jerry Zucker says: 'Nobody else is paying as much attention to your failures as you are . . . To everyone else, it's just a blip on the radar screen, so just move on.' Most overnight successes take about 10 to 15 years, and the journey is not a linear path but rather a series of ups and downs with a major dip along the way known as the 'test'. A test could take the form of bad PR or one of your top performers walking out of the door. Try building risk and resilience into your daily routine. Focus on resilience instead of strength, which means you want to yield and allow failure and you bounce back instead of trying to resist failure. At times, you might privately think you can't go on. You must persist. Arianna Huffington, cofounder of *The Huffington Post*, says it best: 'I failed, many times in my life. One failure that I always remember was when my second book was rejected by 36 publishers. Many years later, I watched *HuffPost* come alive to mixed reviews, including some very negative ones, like the reviewer who called the site "the equivalent of *Gigli*, *Ishtar*, and *Heaven's Gate* rolled into one". But my mother used to tell me, "Failure is not the opposite of success, it's a stepping stone to success."'

Questions:

1. What can you do to build risk and resilience into daily routine?

2. Do you let the fear of failure stop you from embracing change?

3. What steps could you take to build a strong mind for yourself and your team?

Brave is the second dimension of the 3D Leader and is essential to feeling alive at work. It ensures ROI – return on intelligence – from your teams and helps everybody to bring their best and most daring selves to work.

KEY MESSAGES

- The *brave* dimension inspires everybody to feel more alive at work and be their bravest self. How will you enable your employees to bring their best and boldest self to work?

- Psychological safety (curiosity safety, challenger safety, collaboration safety and culture safety) is the biggest driver of the brave dimension. How will you accelerate this across your whole organisation?

- It's impossible to speak up, share ideas and make a difference if psychological safety is low. What will you do to launch, scale and sustain a culture of high psychological safety and high diversity?

- Most teams are not teams. They are just groups of individuals with their own idea of what success looks like. How will you tap the power of quantum teamwork?

- Your team are not mind readers. How will you declare expectations and then inspire and empower the team to deliver against them?

- The language of leadership is the language of empathy. The problem is those who are seen as powerful are often least likely to show empathy. How will you lead with empathy and help your team cultivate it?

- We are blind to our own blindness. How will you flag blind spots and build strengths for your team and self?

- Trust is the foundation of every action, relationship and interaction. How will you prioritise trust alongside growth, learning and talent?

ACTION

If you do only one thing now, ask your team to evaluate the current levels of psychological safety (curiosity safety, challenger safety, collaboration safety and culture safety) and use the findings to flag blind spots, increase team strengths and close gaps.

Websites

www.angeladuckworth.com

www.sisulab.com

https://rework.withgoogle.com

www.instituteofcoaching.org

www.gallup.com

Podcasts

CultureLab with Aga Bajer

Be Afraid and Do It Anyway with Brené Brown

Masters of Scale by Reid Hoffman

The Tony Robbins Podcast

The Mindvalley Podcast

TED Talks

The Power of Vulnerability – Brené Brown

Grit: The Power of Passion and Perseverence – Angela Duckworth

Sisu: Transforming Barriers To Frontiers – Emilia Lahti

The Gift and Power of Emotional Courage – Susan David

Courage is Contagious – Damon Davis

CHAPTER 4

BEYOND

Be legendary.

Nike

In this chapter you will learn to:

- *grow your posse*
- *be the change*
- *walk your why*
- *go beyond.*

Answer these questions. What keeps you awake at night? And are you changing too fast or not fast enough? In our lifetime, technology has advanced at an extraordinary rate. Research by Boston Consulting Group illustrates the time it's taken for each one of the following inventions to reach 100 million users:

- Telephone: 75 years.
- Web: 7 years.
- Facebook: 4 years.
- Instagram: 2 years.
- Pokémon GO: 3 months.

There is really only one way to live in a world of speed, surprise, change and uncertainty, and that's to visit the *beyond* dimension. The beyond dimension is defined as 'how you lead yourself, make relationships, smash your fears and go beyond your limits'. When you truly go beyond, it changes the way you think and act as a leader. You plan and strategise differently. You become an explorer, a gatherer and a creator.

One thing I've learned about the beyond dimension is to grow your posse. Remember that you're the average of the five people you spend the most time with. Think about that for a minute. Ask yourself: who would be in my circle of five? Your posse means that connecting with other inspiring thinkers and doers is just as important as being talented or working hard. Your posse includes co-workers, mentors and sponsors where learning from them will give you a huge advantage. Your leadership heroes are part of your circle, too – read about them, follow them and learn from them. Your posse pushes you to become the leader you wish you had. You have a choice. Are you a bystander watching the world go by or an upstander who thrives on doing the impossible? It all starts with connection.

BORN TO CONNECT

Simon Sinek, author of *Leaders Eat Last*, advocated that connection is not just necessary to our survival as a race but is key if you want to thrive. Connection is as necessary as food, water and shelter. To feel part of something, the team and the vision are incredibly rewarding not just for our well-being but also for doing great work. Community comes from the Latin word *communis*, which means, 'shared gift'. There is a growing body of research led by thinkers such as Wharton School Professor Adam Grant and author Dan Pink that shows that connecting with others is critical for reaching your leadership potential. In his *New York Times* bestseller *Give and Take: Why Helping Others Drives Our Success*, Grant explores workplace dynamics and the value of connection. In a recent McKinsey interview, Grant elaborates: 'All of these flattening structures, these ad hoc collaborations that require improvisation, are, at their core, about interdependence. And the data show that it's in interdependent situations that givers thrive. So if you're the kind of person who enjoys helping others, when you're working in a team, you have the ability to make the team better and really multiply the team's success in a way that, ideally, reverberates to benefit everyone in the team.' What steps are you taking to build meaningful connections inside and outside of your organisation?

CASE STUDY

Marie Schneegans is the founder and CEO of a French startup, Never Eat Alone. The truth is, if you work in a large company, chances are you always eat alone at your desk or have lunch with the same people in your department. It's not easy to meet new people. This is a universal problem for thousands of people around the world: connections are missed, ideas are lost, and the work culture suffers as a result. Never Eat Alone puts an end to this. Its goal is to bring individuals together by using a customised lunch app on your phone. List your background and project interests and you can connect with colleagues who share similar goals. As an employee, you get to proactively reach out to anyone in the company, including the CEO, and for the organisation, it's a great way to build a stronger whole-person culture where people bring more of themselves to work every day.

Questions:

1. How easy is it to meet new people in your organisation?
2. What initiatives do you have in place to engineer serendipity and chance encounters?

DUNBAR'S NUMBER

The number 150 is significant for anyone who wants to be a 3D Leader. It can help you decide where to focus your attention and on whom. Robin Dunbar is the Director of the Institute of Cognitive and Evolutionary Anthropology at Oxford University and the author of *How Many Friends Does One Person Need?* He has spent more than 20 years studying social behaviour and has found that 150 is the optimal number or anthropological limit for the number of meaningful relationships we can have. Dunbar noticed that most tribes have around 150 members, and even armies throughout Western history, from the Roman Empire to the modern-day US military, have around 150 soldiers in a small company.

In an interview in *The Guardian*, he says: 'The way in which our social world is constructed is part and parcel of our biological inheritance. Together with apes and monkeys, we're members of the primate family – and within primates there is a general relationship between the size of the brain and the size of the social group. We fit in a pattern. There are social circles beyond it and layers within – but there is a natural grouping of 150. This is the number of people you can have a relationship with involving trust and obligation – there's some personal history, not just names and faces.'

As with any human trait, there will always be outliers – those who have the capacity to know a lot more people. Now, with the advent of social media sites such as Instagram, it's possible to connect to hundreds, if not thousands, of people. However, it's face-to-face contact where the highest exchanges of trust and respect occur. Dunbar's number can help you organise your collaboration efforts in a more systematic way, saving time and energy:

Checklist

1. Make a list of the key people inside and outside your organisation – that is, those on whom you depend the most to get the job done.

2. Prioritise them in order of importance.

3. Find a mutually beneficial reason to connect.

4. Reach out to them.

5. Sustain your relationships for the long term through reciprocity and generosity.

NAMES NOT NUMBERS

Julia Hobsbawm's impact on the practical study of knowledge networking has made her the world's first professor in networking and an Honorary Visiting Professor at Cass Business School. She is the founder of Editorial Intelligence, a networking business committed to 'developing deeper personal connections and having a more profound understanding of today's information overloaded landscape'. Her flagship event, Names Not Numbers (NNN), is an ideas festival where intellectually curious people come together for learning and inspiration.

According to her latest research, 69.5% of survey respondents agree that 'networking is essential for building and managing a career' and 53.3% strongly agree that 'networking helps productivity because it brings fresh ideas and connections into the workplace'. How should you network smarter? A useful analogy is to imagine your own personal boardroom. Ask yourself: 'Who are the 20 individuals I need to build bridges with over time?' A simple knowledge dashboard is a useful way to stay ahead of the learning curve:

1. Watch (e.g. TED film).

2. Hear (e.g. HBR IdeaCast podcasts).

3. Read long (e.g. *Inc.* Magazine).

4. Read short (e.g. getAbstract or Blinkist).

5. Read inspirational quotes (e.g. www.success.com).

Human to human interaction is still where it's at if leaders want to inspire, grow and empower others. An algorithm cannot trump the power of eye contact, tone of voice and body language that can translate into strong working relationships between people. Hobsbawm says: 'People have been so obsessed with social networks that they really haven't noticed the human side, the non-algorithm side, is still where it's at.'

How should you prepare for intelligent networking to take place? To network smarter, you must break through some cognitive biases that can derail your efforts. Three, in particular, must be understood in order to unlock the benefits of networking:

1. Proximity bias

Most office layouts create invisible walls of resistance for leaders. Today's work environment is often remote, with people working across different time zones, cultures and geographies. The proximity principle is an unconscious bias that influences who you spend the most time with and how much. A director of a global software company, says:

> 'You take for granted where you sit in the office. The truth is that it really matters. When I did an inventory of those whom I trusted the most, I found the majority of my relationships were within my own team and department. Do the test for yourself because it's a big wake-up call.
>
> My success depends on building bridges with people who sit mostly outside my department, such as Sales, Finance and HR. If you leave it to chance, you'll realise that the relationships that need building are the very ones that get neglected. Most leaders are thinking 90% about their own agenda rather than the other person they are trying to connect with. It makes the job more difficult trying to influence a stranger.'

A question many leaders ask me is how long to spend on networking. The answer is: more than you are spending today. A minimum of two hours a week of relevant networking is a sensible starting point.

Checklist

1. Have a plan: make a list of who you know and who you need to know.
2. Start with why: have a reason to say hello and grab a coffee. A strong network means being able to ask for help but also offering it. If you're invisible, you won't even figure on the other person's radar.

3. Look for areas of mutual interest: it's about give and take and creating new opportunities for learning and growth.

4. Activate strong and weak ties: wouldn't the people with whom you have the strongest connection be the most willing to help you? Strong ties are useful for providing job-specific knowledge and information but weak ties are more likely to help you step into new worlds and contexts.

5. Pay attention a few hours a week to connect, growing a wide selection.

6. Be visible: once a week, sit with a different team or swap seats with a peer.

7. Get started: take action to make knowledge networking part of your everyday mindset. The key is to build a wide pool of networks across functions, industries and experiences – diversity is key.

2. The self-similarity bias

Try this test: make a list of the 10 most important people in your network. Chances are, they'll be similar to you in many ways, including in their experience level, education, perspective, status and values. Don't worry, this is perfectly normal – it's called the self-similarity principle. We mostly hang out with people of similar tastes and backgrounds. The problem is that too much similarity in your networks restricts your access to different perspectives, which are vital for creativity and problem solving. It becomes a constraint to thinking differently and can lead to blind spots in your leadership style that go unnoticed until they become a crisis.

David Rock, the founder of the NeuroLeadership Institute, says: 'We've evolved to put people in our in-group and out-group. We put most people in our out-group and a few people in our in-group. It determines whether we care about others. It determines whether we support or attack them. The process is a by-product of our evolutionary history where we lived in small groups and strangers we didn't know well weren't to be trusted. The default setting for most leaders is closed networks where you are connected to people who already know each other.' To combat the self-similarity bias, leaders should take an audit of who's in their in-group and out-group, and then act upon the results.

Ask yourself: to what degree am I activating both strong and weak ties across my networks?

3. Groupthink

Great minds don't think alike. Solomon Asch's conformity experiments in the 1950s offer a strong lesson in the power of groupthink. Asch gave his participants the following task: pick which of three different lines – A, B, or C – was most like the target line. The task was obvious, but there was a catch: out of eight people, only one was a genuine subject and the other seven were close associates of Asch's who had been instructed to unanimously pick a line that did not match. The questions were: 'Would the subject stick to their guns and trust their own eyes?' and 'Would they be swayed by group pressure and conform to the majority view?'

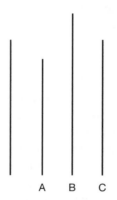

A   B   C

The Asch experiment

Asch measured the number of times the subject conformed to the major- ity view. On average, about a third of the subjects gave in to groupthink, even when the answer was clearly wrong (C was the correct answer). Over all the trials, about 75% of subjects conformed at least once to the incorrect answer and only 25% of subjects never conformed. Why did so many of the subjects doubt their own eyes and agree with the rest of the group? Offered a choice between speaking our mind and fitting in with the group, we opt for fitting into the group almost every time. Social pressure matters more than we imagine it does. We also assume that the group is better informed than us, even when the truth is clear to see. There's nothing more dangerous than a group of minds that are too afraid to tell the truth.

Ask yourself: to defeat groupthink, what measures could I put in place to reward dissent and encourage straight talking at all levels?

CASE STUDY

Did you know that most organisations are made up of I-shaped managers more than a T-shaped leader?

To lead strategically, become T-shaped and think about your role like the letter 'T'. The horizontal part of your 'T' represents strategic focus and horizontal trust across other units of the organisation. There are huge advantages of growing your 'T', from wider leadership impact to silo busting. The vertical part of your 'T' is all about operational focus and vertical trust. You tend to find it more in old command and control cultures. Now, the default style for most people is an I-shaped manager: strong operational focus and vertical trust, but lacking the strategic focus and horizontal trust across other parts of the business.

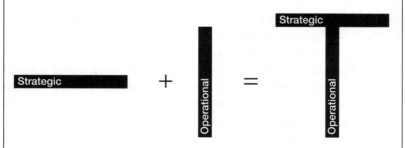

T-shaped versus I-shaped

Specialisation improves efficiency – but it also leads to tunnel vision and HiPPO or excuse cultures. When the speed of change is low, it's possible to succeed as an I-shaped manager and execute on a long-term repeatable business model but now the risk of everybody getting trapped in the same mental silo is too high. What got you to where you are will not get you to where you want to be, however. To lead in the future and be more resilient to massive, yet hard-to-predict change, you must commit to become a T-shaped leader through building up multiple mentors, job rotation and proactively seeking out different perspectives from your own about the forces that are shaping your industry.

▶

The Cleveland Clinic is one example of an organisation that has successfully promoted cross-disciplinary collaboration through helping specialists become more T-shaped. The result is more patient-centred outcomes and deliberate silo busting that replaces 'me' with 'we'.

Questions:

1. Are you an I-shaped or T-shaped leader?
2. How could you grow your T as a leader and a team?
3. What can you do to break down silos across your organisation?

SUPERPOWER CIRCLES

One of your biggest goals as a 3D Leader is to build superpower circles inside and outside of your organisation. Superpower circles are inspired by the creative circles of the French post-impressionists, known as the Société des Artistes Indépendants. Famous artists such as Paul Cézanne, Vincent van Gogh and Georges Seurat came together at cafés in the Parisian suburb of Montparnasse to connect, share ideas and draw upon the wisdom of their peers. Heated debates and even drunken brawls occasionally spilled out onto the street. While I do not condone drunken brawling, I do believe that leaders can be more creative by embracing new experiences, breaking out of old patterns and stepping into the shoes of others more.

In an exclusive *Wired* interview, Steve Jobs expounded on some of the principles of Société des Artistes Indépendants:

> *'Creativity is just connecting things. When you ask creative people how they did something, they feel a little guilty, because they didn't really do it, they just saw something. It seemed obvious to them after a while. That's because they were able to connect experiences they've had and synthesize new things. And the reason they were able to do that was that they've had more experiences or they have thought more about their experiences than other people. A lot of people in our industry haven't had very diverse experiences, so they don't have enough dots to connect, and they end up with very linear solutions without a broad perspective on the problem. The broader one's understanding of the human experience, the better design we will have. When's the last time you stepped into the shoes of somebody else or let go of outdated ways of seeing the world?'*

The 3D Leader leverages five superpower circles that will scale the best version of you:

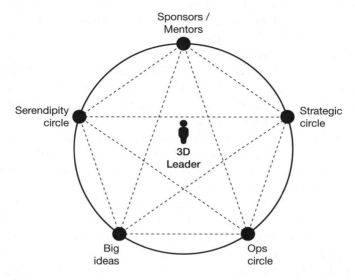

Superpower circles

1. Sponsors and mentors

Why learn from your own mistakes in business when you can learn from someone else's? I'm a big fan of reaching out to sponsors and mentors: they can raise your game as well as build a stronger talent pipeline. In my own company, I've been mentoring a young entrepreneur who recently raised $1.5 million for his own startup and was named in the *Forbes* '30 Under 30' list. I also serve as an entrepreneur mentor at London Business School to help students launch exciting new businesses.

Warren Buffett is a notable mentor to Bill Gates, while Eric Schmidt, former CEO of Google, credits Bill Campbell as one of his mentors and when Steve Jobs passed away, Mark Zuckerberg of Facebook acknowledged that the Apple Founder had been an 'incredibly important mentor'. With the meteoric pace of change, it's essential for leaders to have a private space to reflect and talk through challenges they face. Rockstar Group, for instance, aims to provide that and is blazing a trail in the world of startups. Founded by Jonathan Pfahl, an ex-Goldman Sachs Wealth Manager, Rockstar Group has built a reputation for accelerating leadership success for others.

Sponsors and mentors will help you bolster self-awareness and emotional intelligence – two vital leadership qualities. Every leader has a blind spot, visible to others but not to themselves. Mentors will help you see your blind spot and also give feedback so that you're always thinking about what you can do better. I'd estimate that around 75% of leaders use or plan to use a mentor at some stage. They understand the benefits of working with a mentor. Jack Dorsey, CEO of Square and co-founder of Twitter, credits philanthropist Ray Chambers as one of his closest mentors. A feature in *Business Insider* states that Chambers has said: 'Dorsey has learned to think bigger and better and "at the core of his being, he really wants to make the world a better place".'

A good track record counts for everything. Check their history to see that he or she will bring new learning into the relationship. And don't restrict a mentor to just one. Go for multiple sponsors and mentors. In a *Forbes* interview, former LinkedIn CEO Reid Hoffman concludes that wide and diverse networks can help leaders to see around corners, face adversity and lead in times of unprecedented uncertainty.

You should aim to build a wide circle of sponsors and mentors. Face-to-face contact works best, although this isn't always necessary with the advent of Skype, Zoom and other technologies. Be clear about the difference between mentors and sponsors. In short, mentors guide you and sponsors advocate you:

- Mentors provide help and guidance on a whole range of leadership development goals, including access to useful connections. To a mentor, you are their mentee.

- Sponsors proactively help you advance your career and make your leadership aspirations a reality. To a sponsor, you are their protégé.

When approaching mentors and sponsors, be clear about your leadership development goals and agree to the outcomes at the beginning. A good rule of thumb is to meet once a quarter for up to 90 minutes, with some actionable goals to take away from each session. Having mentors and sponsors is by far one of the most effective ways to accelerate the bold, brave and beyond dimensions of 3D leadership. Approach mentors and sponsors with a clear purpose and you'll be surprised at how many say yes; just don't waste their time. Be crystal clear about your 'why' before introducing yourself.

Questions:

1. Do you have a good balance of sponsors and mentors?
2. What outcomes do you want to achieve by engaging sponsors and mentors?
3. Who could you be a mentor to?

2. Ops circle

Whom do you trust? The Ops circle is where you spend most of your time: it's the job – this means your immediate boss, their boss and your direct team. This is your inner circle, where success will depend on the help and collaboration of others. Trust is key. If you look at how decisions are made, most influencing happens without authority. Other departments will also fit within the Ops circle: human resources, sales, finance, marketing and information technology. You should reach out to those you depend on – an informal coffee together to check in for 15 minutes builds trust, goodwill and strengthens the relationship for reciprocity. Job rotation, cross-functional projects and sitting with another team for half a day are proven ways to sharpen your Ops circle, and stay connected to people and ideas.

Questions:

1. How would you rate the current strength of your Ops circle? What needs to change?
2. What unique skills, knowledge or information could your team share with other parts of the business?

3. Strategic circle

Do you spend more of your time working 'in' the business rather than 'on' the business? A strategic circle is made up of leaders who hold expert status in your industry. They could sit inside and outside of your organisation. They have built up a high profile as opinion leaders; this means that what they say directly impacts your operating environment, how your business runs, or even industry regulations. They may not be in your immediate circle but will exert considerable power over how things get done. They could be leaders, competitors or even your own boss. It's useful to connect to these people on social media sites such as LinkedIn and Twitter. Distill the views of each opinion leader and use them to build up a rich context about the type of world you're leading in today. Most leaders are adept at the operational side of work – after all, that's where you spend most of your energy and time. You have to have an eye on the future as well; this is the big picture as well as the detail. Your strategic circle will give you access to the type of trends and insights that your future self will thank you for.

Questions:

1. Which interesting leaders and people of influence do you follow on social media?
2. How could you bring 'outside' thinking into your organisation on a more regular basis? For example, guest speakers.

4. Big ideas circle

What's your zeitgeist? The big ideas circle is like your very own panel of rebels, non-conformists and change-makers who ask questions that can blow the cobwebs off business as usual. This powerful circle is made up of people who send an electric jolt to your brain when they write and speak. They are scientists, writers, painters, anthropologists, economists and business people. You may not get to meet them in person, but you can certainly get closer to them. Follow them on LinkedIn, watch them on TED, hear them at a conference and read their research, interviews and books. The big ideas circle should shake up your view of the world with surprising insights that transform your mind and your work.

Questions:

1. Who is in your big ideas circle and do they inspire you with new questions?
2. How often do you have diverse experiences that inspire you to think differently about the world?

5. Serendipity circle

Do you believe in luck? Luck is about being prepared for when the opportunity presents itself. In his book *The Luck Factor*, Professor Richard Wiseman of the University of Hertfordshire describes why lucky people tend to share traits that make them luckier than others. This includes the impact of chance opportunities, lucky breaks and being in the right place at the right time. He says: 'My research revealed that lucky people generate good fortune via four basic principles.' The four principles are:

1. They are skilled at creating and noticing chance opportunities.

2. They make lucky decisions by listening to their intuition.

3. They create self-fulfilling prophesies via positive expectations.

4. They adopt a resilient attitude that transforms bad luck into good.

On the flipside, he says: 'Those who think they're unlucky should change their outlook and discover how to generate good fortune. I believe luck is as much about what you expect as what you do. I've tried to be open to luck in my own career and develop serendipity circles. Serendipity is defined as "a passionate curiosity in the world around you". It's a skill and an attitude that should be developed. Most people have remarkable resources at their fingertips, but never figure out how to leverage them. Take advantage of chance encounters, break the weekly routine and, once in a while, have the courage to try something new and step out of your comfort zone. A serendipity circle can change your day or could change your life. The world is full of magic if you're prepared to embrace it.'

Questions:

1. Do you wait for success to happen or do you get out there and make it happen?

2. When was the last time you broke out of the weekly routine or had a chance encounter?

CASE STUDY

How do you build the goodwill of others? Having a trusted network is something no leader should be without. 9others is a borderless entrepreneurial ecosystem that knows ideas travel faster through networks than hierarchies. It was founded

▶

by entrepreneurs Matthew Stafford and Katie Lewis on the belief that 'your success requires the aid of others' and has now grown to a network of over 4,000 people in 45 cities around the world. A host and nine others meet for an informal dinner to mingle, discuss challenges and share experiences. Coming together to understand each other's challenges from different perspectives allows leaders to help each other move forward.

Stafford says: 'A deliberately small group, loosely curated, of entrepreneurs came together, shared a challenge and helped each other out. We didn't know what it would lead to but we instinctively knew that a small gathering of good people would undoubtedly make some good things happen. That's why from now and with your help we are building the Borderless Entrepreneurial Ecosystem needed to support leaders anywhere in the world. It's "Borderless" because it doesn't matter where people happen to be because we're all connected.'

Questions:

1. What could you do to build your own trusted networks that thrive on human connection?
2. How confident are you at networking across different formats, for example, conferences or breakfast briefings?
3. What could you do to raise your leadership profile? For example, speak at an event.

BE THE CHANGE

One of the challenges for every organisation is that technology changes faster than humans do. 3D Leaders asks themselves, 'Am I learning as fast as the world is changing?' Garry Ridge is the CEO of WD-40, the world's leading lubricant company, and is on a mission to keep learning as fast as the world is changing. Over the past 20 years, WD-40's sales have quadrupled and its market cap has increased from $250 million to a little over $2.5 billion. Central to building the beyond dimension, at WD-40 there are 'learning moments', which means hitting the pause button to understand lessons learned and the valuable insights for doing things faster, better or cheaper.

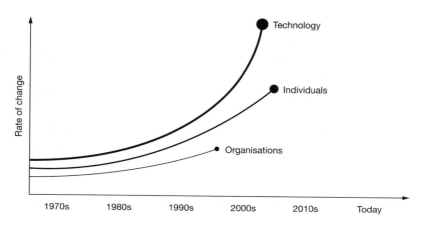

Rate of change

One of Ridge's biggest learning moments in life is three magic words, 'I don't know'. To underscore his commitment to lifelong learning, legend has it that he signs off emails with one of the artist Michelangelo's favourite mottos *'ancora imparo'*, Italian for 'I am still learning'. A learning moment means moving from fear of failure to freedom to fail. It's about learning, experimenting, asking and improvising and is the opposite of a know-it-all culture. A learning moment can be positive or negative, but they are never bad and should always be shared. When was the last time you experienced a learning moment?

Here are three ways to become the change you aspire to be:

1. **Pre-mortem.** An ounce of prevention is worth a pound of cure. At Google, it's common for teams to conduct a pre-mortem before committing time and resources to a project. A pre-mortem is the hypothetical opposite of a post-mortem and follows four simple steps:

   1. Start the exercise by explaining what a pre-mortem is and imagining that the project has failed spectacularly.

   2. Ask everyone to write down every reason they can think of for the failure – especially the kinds of things they ordinarily wouldn't mention as potential problems. Examples include interpersonal conflict, wrong KPIs and too many rules.

   3. Give people a safe space to think. In describing risks and weaknesses that no one else has mentioned, team members feel valued and safe to voice fears and concerns before they

happen. This builds reserves of psychological safety that can be tapped in future.

4. Fight fear with action. In the end, a pre-mortem helps to identify threats to new initiatives and develop a defence against them by talking about it openly and, importantly, can provide the benefits of learning from failure while avoiding the pain of actually failing.

2. **Intelligent failure.** Bill Gates said, 'Never waste a good mistake.' Ask yourself: is failure a badge of honour or a badge of shame in my organisation? To fail intelligently, follow four simple steps:

1. First, know what success looks like and doesn't look like. I'm always surprised at the lack of a clear outcome. Deciding what not to focus on can also limit the uncertainty.

2. Second, convert assumptions into knowledge and learning. This is a much smarter use of time than trying to prove how right you are.

3. Third, codify and share what's been learned with a process known as 'After Action Reviews' (AARs). Pioneered by the military to ensure continuous learning, the process involves asking: 1. What did you intend to happen? 2. What happened? 3. What are the lessons learned?

4. Finally, ask: what is our proudest failure? *Dio Los Muertos* (Day of The Dead) is a way for others to share stories of what went wrong and inspire each other with lessons learned to move forward. While most cultures just talk about success, it helps for leaders to signal to others that behind every success is failure.

3. **Go live from day one.** Organisations such as Shazam and Airbnb empower employees with a sense of pride by giving employees the freedom to push code directly to their platforms as soon as they start working at the companies. The goal is to help everybody think and act like an owner from day one at the company and to signal that they are already empowered to act rather than ask.

Questions:

1. How would you rate levels of ownership in your own team?

2. Do your team members react to or anticipate most problems?

3. To what level is your team empowered to make their own decisions?

RIP UP THE RULEBOOK ON CHANGE

Why is it that leaders with the most success are often the ones who rebel against the status quo? The easiest thing for a leader to do is to react to change, the second easiest thing is to respond and the most difficult thing is to initiate change. The only thing that will change is change.

Change is not easy, but tackling the root of the problem by simplifying the approach and scaling a pro-change mindset will boost the likelihood of success. At Accenture, CEO Julie Sweet says there are five things to keep in mind when going through change:

1. **Clarify vision:** set a clear and ambitious goal that will help you substantially transform your leadership and let it guide your future decisions.

2. **Prioritise change:** transformations are driven by changing customers. Don't kick off all new initiatives at once. Instead, be clear about how the initiatives will be sequenced and how they relate to one another.

3. **Conduct frequent sprints:** kick off the change with frequent sprints (plan, do and review). Take constant reality checks and adapt the plan accordingly. This helps to allocate resources on those areas that contribute the most value.

4. **Adapt or die:** respond to obstacles that emerge during the transformation and course-correct whenever needed.

5. **Less is more:** create a simplified first version of your envisioned end-state that will still deliver a significant amount of impact in the first phase. Change is never easy, and the odds are hardly in any transformation's favour. But tackling the root of the problem by simplifying the design and using a pragmatic approach – through implementation sprints – will boost the likelihood of success.

While we all aim for perfection, we should not fall into the perfection trap, which can stop you from getting started. Instead, practise daily courage and remember that the difference between who you are and who you want to be as a leader is what you *do*.

Questions:

1. Are your employees changing as fast as the external environment changes?

2. As a leader, do you mostly react to change or initiate change?

3. What steps could you take to build a pro-change culture?

CASE STUDY

Ask yourself: do I have a growth mindset or a fixed mindset? Carol Dweck, a Stanford Psychologist, argues that your view of yourself as a leader can determine everything. If you believe that your intelligence is fixed, you will want to prove this belief correct rather than learning from your mistakes and growing. A fixed mindset means you:

- *avoid challenges*
- *give up too easily*
- *ignore feedback*
- *feel threatened by others' success.*

The end result is never achieving your full leadership potential and focusing on limits rather than possibilities.

Alternatively, if you believe your intelligence can be developed throughout your life, you are more likely to adopt a powerful passion for learning and discovery that allows leaders to thrive during some of the most challenging times in their lives. A growth mindset means you:

- *embrace challenges*
- *don't give up too easily*
- *learn from feedback*
- *enjoy solving challenges that stretch you.*

In a TED talk, Dweck says you should spend more time operating in a space just outside of your comfort zone – this is the key to developing a growth mindset. It's also the critical element to deliberate practice. Leaders have to choose between two conflicting mindsets: 'Are you not smart enough to solve it (fixed) or have you just not solved it yet (growth)?'

To scale a growth mindset in your own team, use the BEANS framework:

- ***B****ehaviours: inspire a growth mindset by redesigning structures, workflows and talent strategies around your people.*
- ***E****nable: make work simple, intuitive and growth-led.*
- ***A****lign: align work to passion-led projects – move people to where they can leverage their strengths and where future value is created.*

■ **N**udge: use simple nudges such as automatically enrolling people on training or role modelling to instil a growth mindset.

■ **S**upport: be there for your team in those moments of peak stress and show them that a growth mindset is what makes us human.

RIPPLE INTELLIGENCE

One of the core skills of the beyond dimension is cultivating a way of thinking called 'ripple intelligence'. Ripple intelligence is best defined as 'the ability to see the interactions of business contexts like ripples moving across a pond'. Can you navigate different trends, inflection points and contexts that can disrupt an industry or business, and turn them into opportunity? One of the best ways to develop this intelligence is to step outside your normal orbit and have a point of view about the ideas, trends and issues that keep you awake at night, as well as the ones that excite you. Done well, this can help you anticipate hidden opportunities and catch the next big wave before others do. As uncertainties multiply, so do the opportunities.

Here are three ways to build ripple intelligence, an essential trait for the beyond dimension:

1. HACKATHONS

Hackathons can make you more curious and discovery-driven, for example, by helping you pull ideas together or see problems from a fresh perspective. Steven Johnson, author of *Where Good Ideas Come From*, writes: 'Good ideas boil down to a network of neurons within your brain. This network grows as it is exposed to different environments and different ways of thinking. As you learn and become educated, new networks are being formed. Creativity ultimately happens when you can take pieces of this network and combine them in a unique way.'

Questions:

1. When was the last time you or your team disrupted the status quo?
2. How often does your team get the opportunity to solve work-related problems that get in the way of productivity?

CASE STUDY

Actions eat words for breakfast. The software company Atlassian lives by this principle and is famed for its bold values and willingness to change:

- *Open company, no bullshit.*
- *Play as a team.*
- *Build with heart and balance.*
- *Be the change you seek.*
- *Don't **** with the customer.*

One of the ways Atlassian people play as a team is through 24-hour innovation jams. Innovation jams cleverly gamify the workplace with 24-hour competitions to attack the biggest challenges facing the business, and they bring teams together to look at new and better ways to get work done. As part of the activity, an 'irritations inventory' is compiled to prioritise what's making employees' lives more difficult. As the clock ticks away, ideas must be generated using an agreed-upon framework. When teams are empowered to test an idea, it can be changed or scrapped early in the process. They get real-time feedback and learning on the go. The exercise helps avoid multimillion-dollar mistakes down the road, too. Teams with game-changing ideas are invited to pitch their proposals to the company's board of directors. The winners receive funding and recognition for their contribution. Innovation jams are a useful platform for energising teams and making people feel recognised and valued.

2. FUTURE-FIT TEAMS

Inspired by the scenario planning work at Shell, the oil and gas company, the aim of future-fit teams is to explore plausible visions of the future in order to make better decisions today. As speed capital becomes a huge source of advantage for companies, it's critical that leaders build cultures that can adapt quickly. Led by the top team, they report back their research and findings on a quarterly basis in the form of a lively debate. To improve the quality of the predictions, everyone must be brutally honest. It's OK to be wrong. They admit it and learn from it just as much as they enjoy being right. Apart from building up a talented pool of strategic thinkers, other advantages include team collaboration and a culture of candour. Everybody wins.

There are three future scenarios you can explore with your team by using the Future-Fit tool.

Future-Fit Tool

Scenario	Probable	Plausible	Possible
Time horizon	5 years	10–15 years	15+ years
Outcome	Operational focus	Strategic focus	Long-term vision

Questions:

1. How could you use the Future-Fit tool to plan for different scenarios?
2. Are you allocating the most time, attention, talent and resources on probable, plausible or possible futures?
3. Which future scenarios are your blind spot?
4. How could you use the Future-Fit tool to translate trends into growth opportunities?

3. CURIOSITY

One of the main career implications of the digital revolution is a shift in demand for curiosity. Curiosity is the gap between what you know and what you want to know and is key to scaling companies of all sizes. Scale curiosity and you will, inevitably, become not just more inspired but more nimble at seeing around corners, and planting seeds for game-changing innovation. My research shows, because of rapid change, there is now a premium on curiosity but only 28% of leaders report feeling curious in their day-to-day roles at work and, yet, 93% agree curiosity is a top leadership priority alongside managing growth and talent. So, how do you unlock a curiosity mindset in your organisation? It's useful to think of curiosity in three ways: inner curiosity, other curiosity and outer curiosity.

1. **Inner curiosity:** in *The Half-Life of Facts: Why Everything We Know Has an Expiration Date*, Samuel Arbesman, a Harvard mathematician, writes: 'Knowledge is like radioactivity. If you look at a single atom of uranium, whether it's going to decay – breaking down and unleashing its energy – is highly unpredictable. It might decay in the next second, or you might have to sit and stare at it for thousands, or perhaps even millions, of years before it breaks apart . . . Facts, in the aggregate, have half-lives.' Arbesman concludes: 'Facts change in regular and mathematically understandable ways. And only by knowing the

pattern of our knowledge's evolution can we be better prepared for its change.' To combat the half-life of knowledge, you must search for new ways to build your inner curiosity.

With curiosity comes discovery. The physicist and code breaker Alan Turing recently became the face of the new £50 note. Turing's fearless approach to daunting problems and his lifelong curiosity for solving problems is a hallmark of inner curiosity. How do you unlock childlike curiosity and a hunger of mind to learn new things? The best way to trigger inner curiosity is to focus on a knowledge gap. Be aware of what you don't know, especially if it makes you feel uncomfortable. Embrace discomfort, stay teachable and replace the fear of the unknown with the power of curiosity.

2. **Other curiosity:** you do not become an Olympian by watching events on TV and you do not scale curiosity just by reading about it. How well do you know the people whom you lead? Be curious in your peers and seek to find out more about their goals, fears and dreams. Invest energy in listening not hearing, be fully present in meetings and explore new ways of working together by asking questions such as 'How can we be better than the sum of our parts?' Seeking new information, insights and experiences about each other can help remove the curse of groupthink (everybody thinking the same) and change the way your team work together for the better.

3. **Outer curiosity:** what is the future of X? Outer curiosity is the ability to make observations and have an original point of view on the world around you. Charles Babbage was inspired by his knowledge of the silk-weaving industry to conceive the first computer capable of completing mathematical tasks and when Steve Jobs took that calligraphy class at Reed College, he did not predict that he would use it while designing the first Macintosh computer for Apple.

In a VUCA world, leaders must be more daring and push to the edges of their business because the future is not going to present itself neatly in an Excel spreadsheet. It's never been easier to under-predict or over-predict change. The reason? Most leaders find uncertainty uncomfortable, so we are reluctant to confront it. Leaders and their teams can prepare themselves to think more critically about signals and decisions that might impact the future by thinking more like a futurist. Once you are able to see and hear what's up ahead, risks can be navigated without fear and bold futures can be realised. Look for hidden trends and weak signals from the edge and ask yourself: what must be true to succeed?

Questions:

1. How can you scale inner curiosity, other curiosity and outer curiosity in your organisation?

2. How could you signal to others that curiosity really matters?

3. What metrics and incentives could you put in place to encourage curiosity?

4. When's the last time you discovered something new about your industry?

| CASE STUDY | The Huge Power of Thinking Like a Child |

Paul Lindley is the founder of baby food giant Ella's Kitchen, which he sold to Hain Celestial, for $104 million. According to legend, Lindley's business card shows his job title as 'Ella's Dad'. His book Little Wins: The Huge Power of Thinking Like a Toddler *is a masterclass in how to scale your inner curiosity. I sat down with Lindley to explore three powerful lessons we can learn from releasing our inner child. Here are the main talking points:*

1. Release your inner child

Children excel at play, experimentation and failing fast to learn fast. They show creative courage and are happy to dive right in. They embrace uncertainty and ask provocative questions you would not think to ask yourself. According to Lindley, they're not the only factors that drive success, but perhaps they are some of the most important for the 3D Leader. Remember the Polaroid Instant Camera? It was a simple question by the seven-year-old daughter of physicist Edwin Land that led to one of the most iconic inventions of the twentieth century. She asked, 'Why can't I see a photo immediately when it is taken?' It was this innocent question that led Land on a three-year mission to invent the world's first instant camera.

2. Be clueless

The sad truth is, by the time most people leave college, most of their creativity has been educated out of them. We will always battle it out with the two sides of our brain, creativity on the right, and logic on the left. The left brain is like an 800-pound gorilla that wants to stop you from taking risks. Being clueless about the baby food industry was Lindley's secret weapon, reminding him that sometimes naivety can be a gift, especially when you're seeking faster, better or cheaper ways of doing things. The 'this is how we've always done it' attitude will blind you from seeing new opportunities as well as spotting imminent threats. Break out of the left-brained world of safety by unlearning business as usual and challenging assumptions about the world.

3. Fall in love with problems

One day, Lindley was having breakfast with his three-year-old daughter Ella and realised that baby food could be done better and differently. He had seen food pouches sold in a French supermarket, but they were aimed at adults and were mostly sports recovery drinks. He realised that children could hold onto the pouches and feed themselves, making feeding time more fun and much easier than with a spoon. The take-home message is you can build inner curiosity by making it part of your daily routine and remembering that the future belongs to the leaders who are not afraid to explore it, poke at it, question it and turn it inside out.

Questions:

1. How could you replace a 'this is how we've always done it' attitude with one of curiosity?
2. Which traits of a child (e.g. play, experimentation, questions) could benefit your business?

WALK YOUR WHY

The German philosopher Friedrich Nietzsche wrote: 'He who has a why to live for, can bear almost any how' and historian Studs Terkel said: 'Work is about a search for daily bread, for recognition as well as cash, for astonishment rather than torpor, in short, for a sort of life rather than a Monday through Friday sort of dying.' The 3D Leader is hardwired for purpose. I define purpose as 'your reason for being and motivation to act'. Without a clearly defined 'why', we become less than the sum of our parts. C.R. Snyder, the late psychologist and author of the book *The Psychology of Hope: You Can Get There from Here,* refers to the ability to generate routes to shape the future as 'waypower' (know direction) and the motivation to move along these routes as 'willpower' (determination). Now, look around your own team. Research by Nick Craig and Scott A. Snook, published in the *Harvard Business Review*, found that 'fewer than 20% of leaders have a strong sense of their own individual purpose. Even fewer can distil their leadership purpose into a concrete statement.' Messages get lost in translation and diluted as they flow up and down and across a company. It doesn't help that leaders often have vastly different and conflicting priorities. Craig and Snook conclude: 'It's not what you do, it's how you do your job and why – the strengths and passions you bring to the table no matter where you're seated. Although you may express your purpose in different ways in different contexts, it's what everyone close to you recognizes as uniquely you and would miss most if you were gone.'

Your leadership purpose expresses who you are and what you do; it's about leading with intention and making change happen. The *Harvard Business Review* has named NVIDIA founder and CEO Jensen Huang as the world's top performing CEO. Huang puts his why down to four principles: 1. Be customer obsessed (not market obsessed); 2. Be innovative; 3. Adopt a long-term approach; and 4. *Ikigai* – a Japanese concept that means 'reason for being'. It is not easy to shape the future, but Huang's clear-eyed bold action is paying off. You have to be driven by something. Leadership purpose is not just about giving energy, but it's unleashing other people's energy, which comes from buying into that shared purpose. But if that purpose isn't strong enough in a company, and if you don't walk the talk as a leader, then the rest will not last long.

Here are three reasons for finding your why, your leadership purpose:

1. Purpose gives meaning

Human beings are meaning makers. The most ancient part of our brain, the reptilian brain at the back of our head, finds meaning through purpose. In a McKinsey interview with researcher Adam Grant of the University of Pennsylvania's Wharton Business School, Grant explains why purpose matters more than ever: 'If you look at the data, what most employees are looking for in their jobs is a sense of meaning and purpose. And, when you look at, in turn, what makes work meaningful, what enables people to feel that their daily lives in organizations are significant – more than anything else it's the belief that "My work makes a difference". That "What I do has some kind of benefit or lasting value to other people." And I think this is something a lot of leaders overlook.' Hit pause and ask yourself how well your team understand the difference between the meaning and the impact of their roles – this question starts with you.

2. Purpose clarifies

Purpose is an essential strategic tool for cutting through distractions and engaging those around you to get the job done. Remember, when you say yes to something, you say no to something else. It's easier to waste time when you don't know what your purpose is. Everything at Patagonia is built around its core purpose and values which include causing no unnecessary harm and building products that do no harm to the planet. That big, long-term goal helps leaders at Patagonia filter through the barrage of distractions and guide every big decision they make. This, in turn, helps Patagonia sustain itself during tough times and overcome challenges by remembering its true purpose. Speaking at a conference, CEO Rose Marcario said: 'I've always focused on a couple of things. One is (to) have a clear direction for the company and what we build. And the other is just trying to build the best team possible toward that . . . I think, as a company – having a clear direction on what you are trying to do, and bringing in great people who can execute stuff – then you can do pretty well.'

3. Purpose simplifies

Do you fight complexity with complexity or fight complexity with simplicity? Today, in the age of overload, business is inherently more complex than it has ever been. Yves Morieux, senior partner at strategy consultancy Boston Consulting Group (BCG), has developed an index to show how business complexity has increased sixfold during the past 60 years alone. And organisational complexity (number of procedures, structures, processes, systems, vertical layers and decision approvals) increased by a factor of 35. While most organisations are drowning in data and information overload, purpose allows you to cut through the noise and focus on what's important. It acts as a powerful decision filter. Without purpose, leaders lose their way and end up drowning in complexity.

Why do you get out of bed in the morning? Whatever your answer, you should be clear about it. And, if you're not, be ready to find out. We all want our work to matter. Nothing is a more powerful motivator than to know that you are making a difference in the world. Having a purpose is your call to action and is a catalyst for establishing clear direction for the company. Try to think about the purpose of your own business for a while. Don't be surprised if you cannot identify it, you're not the only one who doesn't know the purpose of his or her organisation. KPMG, one of the big four auditors, recently launched a higher purpose initiative to help employees address this challenge and move away from the idea that they were just a bunch of finance professionals doing a job. Today they are actively involved and openly celebrate their higher purpose by answering the question: 'How can I share the story about how my work and contribution is making a difference in the world?' The initiative turned into a huge success with over 40,000 stories of purpose being shared to date. How could you rethink the meaning of purpose in your own organisation?

CASE STUDY

These days, my reason for getting out of bed is to help leaders around the world bring their best and boldest selves to work. What's your reason for jumping up in the morning? The Japanese have a secret for finding your higher purpose in business and in life. The term ikigai *(pronounced ick-ee-guy) is a Japanese concept that means 'reason for being'. Your* ikigai *can enhance leadership purpose, meaning and a sense of pride in what you do and is at the intersection of four interconnecting circles.*

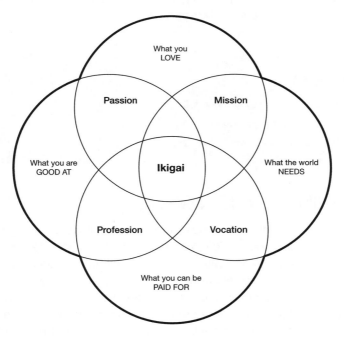

Ikigai

- What you love (your passion).
- What the world needs (your mission).
- What you are good at (your vocation).
- What you can be paid for (your profession).

To discover your own ikigai, *ask yourself the following four questions:*

1. *Am I doing something that I love?*
2. *That the world needs?*
3. *That I am good at?*
4. *And that I can be paid for?*

You can unlock the power of ikigai *only once you know what it is for you. Fill each circle with words, pictures and ideas that fall under each section ('What you love', 'What the world needs', 'What you are good at' and 'What you can be paid for'. Search for the natural overlap of each circle and take your time. That way, your* ikigai *eventually will become clear.*

Questions:

1. How could you use *ikigai* to transform your purpose?
2. Does your team have a clearly defined *ikigai*?
3. What are the risks of not mapping your *ikigai*?

MEANING IS THE NEW MONEY

Social scientist Abraham Maslow's big idea was that we all have a hierarchy of needs: once our basic safety and physiological needs are met, we move to belonging, then status and, finally, self-actualisation. However, this research was completed over 50 years ago and is in need of a major revamp. At Facebook, over 35,000 employees are asked twice a year what they value most at work. After examining thousands of responses, there are three big buckets of motivators that make up the psychological contract: cause, career and community.

- **Bucket one: cause** is about purpose, meaning and autonomy. It's a source of pride in what you do and a sense that your work matters and makes a difference beyond making money.

- **Bucket two: career** is about meaningful work that allows you to play to your strengths and become the best version of yourself. It encourages learning, growth and experimentation and is a key driver of self-motivation.

- **Bucket three: community** is feeling part of something important and drives a sense of what the late psychologist Oliver Sacks called believing, belonging and bonding.

Everybody is searching for their 'who', 'what' and 'why'. The three buckets can be used to help attract and retain your top talent, no matter where you are in the world. Most organisations just prioritise one bucket at the expense of the other two. This is a mistake. When it comes to achieving commitment, most of us are looking for a cause, a career and a community.

Questions:

1. How could you use the three buckets (cause, career and community) to boost commitment and contribution?
2. Which buckets are missing in your organisation?
3. Which buckets do your employees value the most?
4. How can you ensure the company values are put to work every day?

| CASE STUDY | Bold Leaps |

Whatever your view of Elon Musk, it's hard to disagree with his commitment to a bold leaps approach to leadership. In 2019, Musk tied for the No.1 spot for Forbes ranking of America's Most Innovative Leaders. Now, in his early forties, he is a role model for people around the world who want to change the world. For Musk, that means instilling everybody with an exciting purpose and providing deeply meaningful work that gives both urgency and pride. Musk says: 'Big problems attract big thinkers. You have to have a very compelling goal for the company. If you put yourself in the shoes of someone who's talented at a world-class level, they have to believe that there's potential for a great outcome and believe in the leader of the company, that you're the right person to work with.'

Musk is on a mission to revolutionise transportation both on Earth and in space. His automaker, Tesla, which he founded in 2003, has sold more than 280,000 all-electric vehicles worldwide so far. His rocket company, SpaceX, is valued at more than $20 billion and its stated mission is to explore the frontiers of space and ultimately to enable people to live on other planets.

Musk believes that many of the most pressing challenges our planet faces today, from climate change to wildlife loss, are not because of a lack of money

▶

but because of a lack of purpose – that is your reason for being. Think about it. We all know what we do and most of us know how to do it, but only a few leaders know why they do what they do. I can relate to this from working in the advertising industry where I realised that most of the clients I was advising put profit before people. Walking your why, your leadership purpose doesn't happen overnight. Rather, as Musk shows, you must commit time, energy and resources to finding your true purpose by focusing on both willpower and waypower:

1. Willpower: this means the determination to not give up. For Musk, if it's something you're truly curious about, it will prioritise itself. To make your own mark, you must first match your 'why' with focus and effort, then a chemical reaction will start that will enable rapid growth beyond anything you thought possible.

2. Waypower: this means knowing where you are going and having a clear line of sight to get there. For Musk, the lesson is:

$$willpower + waypower = the\ key\ that\ unlocks\ the$$
$$door\ to\ walking\ your\ why.$$

Questions:

1. How would you rate the levels of willpower and waypower for you and your team?

2. Is your purpose motivating? If not, why not?

3. How would you rate your organisation's purpose? Does it give you pride?

GO BEYOND

Finding mentors, continuous improvement, and even chance meetings are telltale attributes of the beyond dimension for leaders. Step outside your normal circle and meet someone new with a different background from your own. This is based upon the ancient Chinese proverb: 'A single conversation across the table with a wise person is worth a month's study of books.' Travel to an unfamiliar destination. Attend a great talk or even watch one on TED. Researcher Liz Wiseman says: 'If you are at the top of your game, it might be time to position yourself at the bottom of the learning curve.'

To accelerate the *beyond* dimension, do more of this:

1. Lead with why

WhatsApp's founder Jan Koum recently departed from Facebook due to disagreements about its purpose and long-term vision for user data privacy and encryption. His journey is a testament to the power of purpose. If staying true to your why, your purpose in life sometimes means being selfish, so be it. Koum showed he had the courage to move on when Facebook's strategy was no longer in sync with his vision for WhatsApp. A clear leadership purpose helps you say no to the wrong things so you can spend more time doing the right things. It's not just about making better decisions. Koum's sudden departure from Facebook shows us why sometimes saying no or even walking away is the best strategy when you are no longer staying true to your purpose.

Do you use your purpose as a filter for making better decisions?

2. Let bad leaders go

Poor leaders cause pain on multiple levels. Employees typically leave a company for one of three reasons, or a combination of them. The first is that they don't feel a connection to the vision of the company, or sense that their work really matters. The second is that they don't trust or respect their team. The third is they have a terrible boss – and this is the biggest reason. New findings from Stanford Graduate School of Business reveal that replacing a poor leader with a good one can generate up to 30% more output from teams. It's a surprising truth and a big wake-up call for everyone.

Which leaders around you need to up their game and why?

3. Find a mentor

Aaron Levie is a big fan of reaching out to mentors. He is the co-founder of Box, the leading enterprise tech company that opened on the NYSE with a market cap of nearly $3 billion. In the early years, before setting up Box, Levie worked hard to find mentors and big-name leaders for advice. Levie says: 'There's no risk in somebody not responding to your email. The cool thing about Silicon Valley – and this is something that is remarkable about this ecosystem – is the mentorship network, the appreciation I think everybody has for the fight and struggle of building companies. I've benefited greatly from people who had built enterprise software companies or just big companies in general, and they were very helpful in the kind of things we should watch out for, the kind of things we should optimise for, and how to build an organisation that can last as long as possible.' A good mentor will:

- push you harder than you expected
- guide you with better questions
- expect continuous improvement
- dare you to dream big
- challenge assumptions
- be a lifelong student and, most importantly,
- teach you how to think, not what to think.

Who do you know or would like to know that could become a sponsor or mentor?

4. Leaders are learners

What's your 'quake' book? This means a book you have read that has shaken up everything you know about the world to its core. Mine is Victor Frankl's *Man's Search for Meaning* because it showed me that hope is the sparkplug of all action. Reading builds cognitive skills, problem solving and creativity – all of which are essential for leading in an era of relentless change. It can also provide new insights and fresh perspectives that help fuel your talent's growth. Try the getAbstract app. It provides five-page executive summaries of books and is a go-to learning tool among top leaders. What books are most inspiring in your own leadership journey?

5. Engineer serendipity

You can grow your luck quotient by being more forward looking, buoyant and proactive as a leader. Take the initiative and do something new every day. The self-similarity principle draws us towards like-minded people who share similar values and mindsets about the world. While this is a comfortable default setting, it can also lead to mental silos and less opportunity to explore fresh perspectives essential for the beyond dimension. Some of the biggest enemies of luck are routine, a closed mind and boredom. I agree with Nobel Prize winning Biochemist Albert Szent-Györgyi, who says: 'A discovery is said to be an accident meeting a prepared mind.' How will you engineer serendipity in your own leadership?

KEY MESSAGES

- You are a natural born learner. To be the change, you must be in a continuous state of learning and growth. Ask yourself: am I a learner or a knower?

- Never eat alone. Build your superpower circles in order to grow as a leader. Ask yourself: which superpower circles need the most attention?

- To collaborate wider and deeper, become a T-shaped leader and build a T-shaped team. Ask yourself: am I an I-shaped manager or a T-shaped leader?

- Purpose is your source code for meaning and impact. Ask yourself: am I exceeding, meeting or falling behind on it?

- There are three buckets you must address to scale the best version of you and your team. They are cause, career and community. Ask yourself: which buckets need improving?

- The best leaders use an alchemy of willpower (determination) and waypower (direction) to get things done. Ask yourself: what levels are my willpower and waypower?

- Replace passion with curiosity, which is the gap between what you know and what you want to know. Ask yourself: how often do I get to follow my curiosity at work?

- To accelerate your leadership journey, build ties with both sponsors and mentors. Ask yourself: do I have a plan to grow my networks or let it happen by accident?

ACTION

If you do only one thing now, ask your team if they are exceeding, meeting or falling behind on their team purpose and decide what steps you need to take to bring people together.

Websites

www.hbr.org

www.forbes.com

www.eonetwork.org

www.influenceatwork.com

www.startwithwhy.com

Podcasts

Tiny Leaps, Big Changes with Gregg Clunis

The Thrive Global Podcast with Arianna Huffington

The 1-3-20 Podcast with Daniel Pink

Squeezing The Orange Podcast with Professor Dan Cable

The Business Lab Podcast with MIT Technology Review

TED Talks

Smash Fear, Learn Anything – Tim Ferriss

The Power of Introverts – Susan Cain

How Great Leaders Inspire Action – Simon Sinek

Do Schools Kill Creativity? – Sir Ken Robinson

The Power of Believing That You Can Improve – Carol Dweck

CHAPTER 5

CONCLUSION: NEXT STEP ACTIONS

Dream big, start small, but most of all, start.

Simon Sinek

In this chapter you will learn to:

- *focus like an F1 driver*
- *lead fast and slow*
- *get started.*

So, there you have it. You now have the tools to launch 3D leadership and benefit from the dimensions of bold, brave and beyond. However, how do you move from knowing to doing? What are the challenges you must overcome to stand a good chance of becoming a 3D Leader?

One of the biggest obstacles to 3D leadership is our diminishing attention span. Leaders are under pressure to do things more quickly and many work hard to answer every request as fast as possible. And, though the mobile phone is by far one of the best inventions of the last century, I believe it is one of the biggest threats to our personal productivity. There are only 480 minutes in an 8-hour workday and 960 months is only 80 years of age: time is life. Leaders are spending more time than they invest reacting to emails, wasting time in meetings, dealing with interruptions and incessantly checking their mobile phones. The risk is that 90% of the day becomes reactive, with no time for strategic thinking, growing the business and leadership. Ask yourself, as a leader: the attention I give to others is probably the rarest and purest form of generosity today, am I ready to give it?

BATTLES FOR ATTENTION

- The average leader receives about 121 emails per day.
- We spend 30–50% of our time in meetings and about 60% of them are considered pointless.
- Only 1 in 3 leaders say they're able to effectively prioritise their tasks.
- We spend, on average, almost 6 hours per day on digital devices.
- 40% of leaders feel exhausted.

Psychologist Herbert A. Simon wrote presciently, over 30 years ago, 'A wealth of information creates a poverty of attention'. There are over 3 million apps in one of the world's leading app stores, many of us check our smartphones once every 6 minutes and most of us carry our digital devices for 22 hours per day. The challenge is that leadership focus is suffering. We are all consumed by 'the cult of accessibility', and leaders are no exception. The people who need to pay attention the most are often the most at risk of distraction. The people who need to focus are often the most fatigued:

- Change fatigue.
- Email fatigue.
- Meeting fatigue.
- Interruption fatigue.
- Collaboration fatigue.

When you operate at such a high level of intensity for too long, you run the risk of running your mental and emotional reserves into the red. It's like a ticking time bomb. The brain floods the body with chemicals such as cortisol and noradrenaline. Primitive instincts take over, forcing the brain into fight, flight or freeze behaviours, what the psychologist Dr Steve Peters calls the 'inner chimp'. For an overloaded leader, this can erode focus and strategic perspective – essential qualities for success.

EXERCISE

Try this exercise, which will take less than a minute: the Apple logo is one of the most recognised and iconic in the world. It is bold and distinct – one of the best in modern design. It's quite likely you own an Apple product or know somebody who does. We see the logo all the time, but do we remember it? If I asked you how confident you are at drawing the Apple logo, how would you reply? Confident? Without peeking, draw the logo. Now, check your drawing with the official Apple logo. How did you do? In a study on attention and recall featured in the Quarterly Journal of Experimental Psychology, *researchers found that only 1 out of 85 participants could recall the logo without any errors. There was a striking difference between participants' confidence levels before the test and the actual results. I was surprised when I got it wrong, too.*

So, what steps can you take to turn talk into action and become the leader you wish you had?

1. Avoid burnout

People don't burn out because of what they do. They burn out because they forget why they do it. According to a recent global survey by LinkedIn, a whopping 89% of people say they don't achieve their daily goals and multi-tasking eats 40% of their day. At many companies, people suffer from collaboration overload where they spend around 80% of their time in meetings or answering colleagues' requests, leaving little time for all the critical work they must complete on their own. The Japanese have a saying for this – *karoshi* that literally means 'death from overwork'. This is a fate we should avoid at all costs.

Ask yourself: do I feel more or less in control than I did last year?

2. Say no fast and mean it

The word 'urgent' is one of the most overused words in the English language. It forces leaders everywhere to become trapped by knee-jerk cultures that simply react rather than think. Try using a range of filters first to evaluate whether the demand is the best use of your time and talent. Effective leaders are masters at protecting their time in order to get things done. They manage expectations based on reality, not fiction, and are skilled at the art of saying no to demands that are presented as urgent but are, in fact, ill-thought-out requests that will waste their day and deplete their energy.

Ask yourself: do I use 'no' as a strategic tool to cut through distractions?

3. Protect time

The 3D Leader protects their time like money: and knows the difference between shallow work and deep work first discovered by author Cal Newport:

- **Shallow work:** anything that doesn't require uninterrupted concentration. This includes most routine repetitive tasks like responding to email and scheduling meetings.

- **Deep work:** the ability to focus without distraction on a cognitively demanding task such as strategic planning or a performance review.

To protect yourself, think of it as either a time debt or a time credit. You run a time debt when you put essential tasks off and spend more time on shallow work. Not taking strategic pause to think ahead will increase a time debt, which you will have to repay later in the form of stress, knee-jerk reactions and poor decision making. Conversely, a time credit is where you automate routine tasks and free up energy to focus on deep work versus shallow work. Remember – busy is a choice, productive is a choice.

Ask yourself: do I protect my time or do I just give it away to other people without managing their expectations? How much time do I spend on shallow work versus deep work?

4. Plan backwards

Do you plan backwards from the future? Planning is like taking your mind to the gym. More important than what leaders decide to implement is what they have the courage to eliminate. They understand that they can't win everything. Venture capitalist John Doerr advises that: 'Ideas are precious, but they're relatively easy. It's execution that's everything.' This may seem obvious, but most leaders try to do too much. You have to decide what to say no to and agree to new plans only if your mind and heart say yes, but this is no easy feat when everything appears urgent.

Once this is clear, remember to plan backward:

1. Figure out what it will take to win.
2. Work back from step one to where you are today.
3. Create a plan to close the gap.
4. Think of your time as money.
5. Execute objectives and key results (OKRs).

Ask yourself: do I take time to plan backwards or allow issues to become emergencies?

5. Stop managing time, start managing focus

I've always focused on a couple of things. One is to have a clear direction for the company and what we build. And the other is just trying to build the best team possible towards that . . . I think, as a company – having a clear direction on what you are trying to do, and bringing in great people who can execute stuff – then you can do pretty well. Daniel Goleman, in his book *Focus: The Hidden Driver of Excellence*, outlines three types of focus for a leader: inner (self-awareness), outer (business context) and other (relationships). Inner focus is about holding a leadership mirror up to yourself. What are your strengths and blind spots? Outer focus is key for understanding the bigger picture: what forces are disrupting your industry? Other focus is about emotional intelligence and social skills, which are useful for building social capital. You can spend more time on 3D leadership if you remove the barriers to becoming one. More important than what leaders decide to implement is what they have the courage to eliminate.

Ask yourself: what am I prepared to stop doing?

6. Lead fast and slow

Pivoting quickly between fast and slow is a universal challenge for any leader: lead too quickly and you risk burnout; take too long and you miss the best opportunities. The dominant rhetoric is of accelerated change. And because the rate of change in the outside world is perceived to be getting greater, the assumption is that we should do so on the inside, too. Sometimes, this creates problems, for example email traffic for its own sake. Every leader needs both fast and slow. The problem comes when there is too much of one and not enough of the other. 'There are two different speeds underlying any business, but some organisations default to fast and some to slow. You have to go out of your way to change that speed.' To lead fast and slow, do the following:

Lead fast:
- Do what gets the fastest result first.
- Designate a delegation hour – have a prompt in your calendar to let go.
- Beat procrastination by starting quickly.
- Become comfortable with imperfection.
- Look for coachable moments in your day.
- Doubt kills ideas, so prototype quickly.
- Communicate often.
- Keep starting until you really start.
- Celebrate success.
- Do less, then obsess.

Lead slow:
- Hire slowly.
- Listen loudly.
- Play for the long game.
- Invest in prevention.
- Earn trust daily.
- Remain objective.

- Build 'alone zones' for thinking.
- Unplug – it's impossible to be creative on demand.
- Protect time.
- Take brain breaks.
- Do less, better.

Ask yourself: how well do I pivot between leading fast and leading slow?

7. Think like an F1 driver

Formula 1 is the most fascinating laboratory for leaders who want to thrive under pressure. On the face of it, Formula 1 champions such as Lewis Hamilton or Sebastian Vettel and leaders might have nothing in common, other than the fact that they do their jobs sitting down, but, in reality, their lives are very similar. Thriving under pressure, constant travelling, lack of exercise and sleep, and dealing with uncertainty can easily overwhelm the brain's cognitive limits unless you put well-being at the core of everything you do. What can you learn from an F1 driver?

1. Ops – time to focus on work-related tasks.
2. Strategic time – time to think about the bigger picture.
3. Renewal time – time to reflect and renew.

As a leader, there will always be battles for your attention.

Ask yourself: do I have a good balance across Ops time, strategic time and renewal time? If not, what's the one thing I should stop and start?

BRAVE NEW YOU

Are you ready to scale the best version of you? The job of the 3D Leader, first and foremost, is to inspire people who are willing to think beyond the status quo. As more business models fail, leaders will be needed for finding original new ways to reinvent themselves and their organisations. Everyone can benefit from being curious, learning to adapt and being nimble at changing direction. Leadership success equals talent, luck and hard work but also breadth. It's a bit like having lots of apps open in your brain so you can make surprising connections, thinking differently and solving problems for the first time. There are firsts for everything. First steps. First words. First person on the Moon. The first of anything is exciting – momentous, even. You can say 'I was there at the start.' This is courage over caution. It's enough to get started. This is 3D leadership.

KEY MESSAGES

- The 3D Leader plays the infinite game. Don't just focus on career, focus on legacy.

- What you do is who you are: track your best work versus your busy work by writing down everything you do and looking at time spent on higher value work versus lower value work.

- Have a 'no' strategy in order to protect your time and get work done.

- Take brain breaks and time out to recharge.

- Attention is the rarest and purest form of generosity.

CHAPTER 6

THE 3D LEADER TEST

In this chapter you will learn to:

- *complete the 3D Leader Test*
- *flag your strengths, gaps and blind spots*
- *launch, scale and sustain 3D leadership*
- *focus on legacy, not just career.*

We live in an age of intense disruption and change, with its challenges and its opportunities. But how do you successfully lead through this change? Take the 3D Leader Test again once you've finished reading the book and see your scores go up. Even better, get somebody who knows you well to take the test on your behalf.

For each dimension, score your strength levels on a scale from 1 (low) to 10 (high). A score of 7 or below for each of the statements indicates a priority area for improvement.

BOLD DIMENSION

1. I have a bold vision of the future.

   1   2   3   4   5   6   7   8   9   10

2. I use failure as a rapid learning tool.

   1   2   3   4   5   6   7   8   9   10

3. I operate with a strong results orientation.

   1   2   3   4   5   6   7   8   9   10

4. I prototype ideas and test them quickly.

   1   2   3   4   5   6   7   8   9   10

5. I understand VUCA.

   1   2   3   4   5   6   7   8   9   10

6. I look outside my industry for inspiration.

   1   2   3   4   5   6   7   8   9   10

7. I am resilient in the face of setbacks.

   1   2   3   4   5   6   7   8   9   10

8. I understand the principles of 10x thinking.

   1   2   3   4   5   6   7   8   9   10

9. I think like an entrepreneur.

   1   2   3   4   5   6   7   8   9   10

10. I am a bold thinker.

   1   2   3   4   5   6   7   8   9   10

Bold total _____ **/ 10 =**

BRAVE DIMENSION

1. I speak up about issues that matter.

   1   2   3   4   5   6   7   8   9   10

2. I build psychological safety in my teams.

   1   2   3   4   5   6   7   8   9   10

3. I give frequently, timely feedback.

   1   2   3   4   5   6   7   8   9   10

4. I encourage constructive debate.

   1   2   3   4   5   6   7   8   9   10

5. I hire for culture contribution.

   1   2   3   4   5   6   7   8   9   10

6. I am committed to silo busting.

   1   2   3   4   5   6   7   8   9   10

7. I build high trust teams.

   1   2   3   4   5   6   7   8   9   10

8. I bring my best self to work.

   1   2   3   4   5   6   7   8   9   10

9. I lead with empathy.

   1   2   3   4   5   6   7   8   9   10

10. I ask brave questions.

   1   2   3   4   5   6   7   8   9   10

Brave total _____ / 10 =

BEYOND DIMENSION

1. I use mentors to raise my game.

   1   2   3   4   5   6   7   8   9   10

2. I am proactive at growing my networks.

   1   2   3   4   5   6   7   8   9   10

3. I never stop learning.

   1   2   3   4   5   6   7   8   9   10

4. I am passionately curious about the future.

   1   2   3   4   5   6   7   8   9   10

5. I lead change.

   1   2   3   4   5   6   7   8   9   10

6. I know my leadership strengths and blind spots.

   1   2   3   4   5   6   7   8   9   10

7. I have a clearly defined leadership purpose.

   1   2   3   4   5   6   7   8   9   10

8. I focus on my best work more than busy work.

   1   2   3   4   5   6   7   8   9   10

9. I think and act like a leader.

   1   2   3   4   5   6   7   8   9   10

10. I challenge the status quo.

   1   2   3   4   5   6   7   8   9   10

Beyond total _____ / 10 =

INDEX